Get A GRIP On Your Dream

---

12 Ways to
Squeeze More
Success Out
of Your Goals

Peter Jeff

GET A GRIP
ON YOUR DREAM

Peter F. Jeff

Copyright © 2002 by Peter F. Jeff
(616)455-GRIP (4747)
www.gripleadership.com
e-mail: GRIPguy@attibi.com

ISBN 0-938716-63-8

Published by
Possibility Press
e-mail: posspress@aol.com
www.possibilitypress.com

Manufactured in the United States of America

Acknowledgements

What is a champion? We usually think of champions as those sports heroes or the business people who claim king-of-the-hill status with their outstanding talents.

But a champion is so much more. A champion is "one who acts or speaks on behalf of a person or a cause." My friend and colleague, Bill Dombrowski, shared that definition with me after I had helped him achieve a goal. I had championed his effort.

Bill had that definition printed on a piece of cardboard for me, and I pinned it up on my office wall. I didn't know it at the time, but that gesture planted the seed that later blossomed into this book. Bill recognized something in me I hadn't—a penchant to help the cause of others, to champion their efforts, and to help bring out the best in them. Thank you Bill!

My hope in writing this book is to champion *your* goals; to champion you in building your business or profession; in enhancing the quality of your life; and in getting a grip on your personal leadership and your dream.

I have had my own champions during my eight years of research and development for this book: my wife, Debbie, and my parents, Frank and Marie Jeff. Thank you all.

Champion —
one who acts or
speaks on
behalf of a
person or a
cause.

Contents

GRIP

*G*oal-setting, *R*isk-making, *I*nitiating and *P*ersisting

G RIP is a process, a system, a tool you can use to get a hold of your dream. GRIP stands for effective *Goal-setting, Risk-making, Initiating and Persisting*. Think of this system as having four distinct but well-linked parts that need to be mastered progressively.

To give you an idea how this system works, picture yourself as a batter in a baseball game. First you step up to the plate. Your goal is to get on first base. From there you risk your way to scoring on second base. Then you initiate your way to third base, and finally you persist and score.

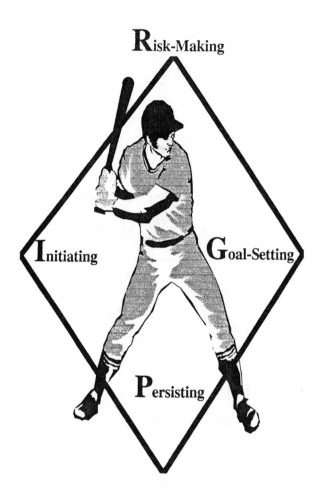

In life, too many people attempt to score before they have successfully even reached first base. Too many people get caught stealing second base when they take dangerous chances instead of calculated risks. Too many people try to hit a home run instead of simply hitting the ball—solidly. And instead of achieving that goal, they often strike out. Strike back with the GRIP system and you will come to an empowering understanding of:

*G*oal-setting...

>as a linkage to purpose and passion;

*R*isk-making...

>as a learning experience;

*I*nitiating...

>as a method to adapt or adjust to changing conditions; and

*P*ersisting...

>as a leadership role to continuously improve.

Use this GRIP process to extend your reach. Break your own sound barriers. Become like Chuck Yeager, the first person to fly faster than the speed of sound. The night before he would boom his way into the history books, Yeager fell off a horse. His shoulder hurt so much the next morning he could not reach up to close his airplane's hatch after he got seated in the cockpit. But Chuck Yeager had a GRIP on his dream to break the sound barrier. He used a broom handle to extend his reach. So he closed the hatch and launched a new era in aviation.

This book can be *your* broom handle. Grip it to close the hatches and sweep away any clutter in your life. Grip it to give birth to your goals after you get a GRIP on your dream—through a system of *Goal-setting, Risk-making, Initiating and Persisting* that will enhance your personal leadership ability.

Part I of the GRIP system includes Yearning, Passion and Conception. *So let's get started!*

Chapter 1

Yearning

Stoking Your Fire

G oals. The business leader quickly scrawled the word goals on the marker board. The letters were so jammed together that goals looked very much like the word gods. That Freudian slip was not lost on the strategic planners attending a goal-setting business meeting. Like religion, goals are often infused with a dogma and a fervor that inspires a martyr-like dedication to the hallowed script of goal-setting—the infamous *to do* list.

But *effective* goal-setting begins first with a more purposeful *Due To* list—a list comprised of long-range commitments that bring your goals into a clearer, more realistic focus. A *due to* list keeps your goals on track, well connected to the Train of Thought and fully linked to the Engine of Purpose. Effective goal-setting is a process of linking (not just listing) the things that will drive you to take certain actions that will help you get your desired results.

For example, *due to* the value I place on hiking and swimming with my grandchildren each summer, I will lose 40 pounds in 20 weeks. The *due to* (enjoying grandchildren) drives the *to do* action step (swimming and hiking) which leads to the desired result (losing weight). And the power of purpose links the two and keeps your train of thought on track to reach your goal or dream.

Yearning Leads to Earning

The power of your desire for your purpose—your *yearning* power—establishes your earning power. To cash in on your goal of earning a high income, you need to first demonstrate that you are a high-powered yearner.

You need to have an urgent longing—as the dictionary defines yearning. And you need to define your goal in the compelling language of something that is *due* you— something you have invested in over time and you're now ready to cash-in on it.

To earn that right, you need to commit to a long-range process of investing in yourself and your passions. Then commit to cashing in that promissory note to yourself. When you learn to yearn with date-certain expectations of success, you will learn to earn more thoroughly than you ever thought possible.

How do you determine what you need to yearn? First you need to define your values. Think of *VALUES* as a word that stands for:

> *Vital Assessment Leveraging Unique Expectations Systematically*

Whatever you assess as being vital, you will systematically develop and nurture. If being healthy is a primary value of yours, you will eat balanced meals and exercise regularly.

Your Bridge to Success

Values drive expectations. Values shape your passion and purpose. Values are the foundation for your Bridge to Success. Your values are imbedded deeply and indelibly into

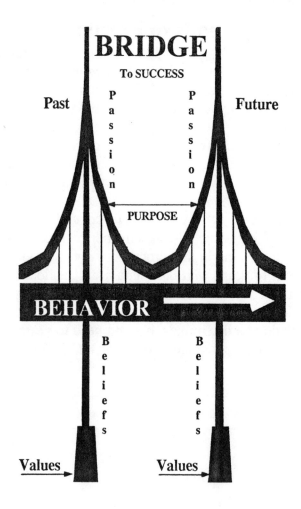

the bedrock of your heart and soul, far below the surface of your feelings.

Your deeply-held values form a foundation that cements your beliefs. And your beliefs, anchored deeply in your values, thrust upward giving birth to the twin towers of passion.

From those towers of passion, your cables of purpose are suspended to create your Bridge to Success. These cables of your commitment are so strong they uphold your behavior and enhance your ability to cross the bridge.

With your values well-defined and with your *due to* yearnings well-aligned, you will more purposely, precisely and powerfully earn your way across the Bridge to Success.

Study the Bridge to Success model on the previous page. You will see how your values uphold your behavior so that you can enhance your ability to *get a GRIP on your dream.* After you've studied the model, then you'll be ready to focus on how you can better develop your values.

Your Wheel of Personal Fortune

You can begin developing your values by spinning your Wheel of Personal Fortune. This will help you determine what tangible results you yearn for—more money, a new house, a new car, better health, more education, more vacation time, etc.

With your vision of your personal fortune—something you have an intense need or craving for, something you are *yearning* for—you will be able to set goals more effectively and efficiently. You will be able to create a healthy tension within yourself to not only define, but also to align your goals to achieve the success you're after. That's what professional golfer Byron Nelson did when he spun his Wheel of Personal Fortune.

Like all effective goal-setters, Nelson knew yearning created the necessary tension to spur his performance. He yearned for a debt-free ranch, and he earned it. In 1945 he won a record 11 professional tournaments in a row, which gave him the necessary funds to attain his goal. Every time he thought of not achieving his goal, it spurred him on even more.

Tension Makes Achievement Possible

Tension strengthens leaders much like it strengthens bridges. The greater the tension, the greater the strength—just like a trampoline that garners opposing forces to stretch and tighten its surface. In fact, the word tension stems from the Latin *tendere*—to stretch.

Yearning goal-setters know that tension can be comforting. In Colonial days, ropes tied to the bed frame suspended mattresses. In order to sleep tight, a person would use a tool to tighten the ropes, strengthen the tension and enhance the comfort of the mattress.

Yearning goal-setters know tension can be nurturing. With tension, the muscles in the human body pull on the bones during exercise, which improves strength. With tension, you relax the muscle fibers that resemble coils of interlocking brushes. Tense the coil and you release the brushes. Tension then spurs greater blood flow, causing more nutrients to go to the cells of the body, and health is improved. Without off-and-on tension in your 625 muscles, they would atrophy.

Yearning goal-setters know tension can spur greater mental prowess. "Mental health is based on a certain degree of tension, the tension between what one has achieved and what one still ought to accomplish, or the gap between what one is and what one can become," said the late, world renowned Dr. Viktor Frankl, former professor of psychology at the University of Vienna.

Yearning goal-setters know tension sparks action, as Martin Luther King Jr. said—"Just as Socrates felt it was necessary to create a tension in the mind so that individuals would rise from the bondage of myths and half truths... so must we create the kind of tension in society that will help men rise from the dark depths of prejudice."

Yearning goal-setters know tension makes achievement possible. As someone wise once said, "No horse does something useful until he is harnessed. No engine ever drives anything until its power is put against a resistance. Niagara Falls cannot turn its falling water into electricity until it encounters the resistance of a generator. No life ever grows great until it is focused, dedicated and disciplined." And no goal is ever achieved unless you create tension. You can unleash that tension by first spinning your Wheel of Personal Fortune.

Spin Your Wheel of Personal Fortune

If people don't spin their Wheel of Personal Fortune before setting their goals, they could end up just spinning their wheels—burying themselves in a rut or gunning their engine with a meaningless list of things to do. In the end, they wind up with nothing meaningful done toward their goals, just the mundane everyday tasks that perhaps someone else could do, or worse yet, with something done that wasted their time, effort and money. How about you? Is it time to take stock of what you're *really doing* with the time you've been given each day? Are you spinning your wheels?

Consider the man who loses 250 pounds in six weeks at a weight loss clinic. He accomplishes his task—his to do list. But eight weeks later he gains back all the weight he lost *plus* 50 pounds, for a total of 300 pounds. Why? "He focused on too narrow a goal," notes the patient's physician, "Now we are helping him review his entire lifestyle, including his beliefs about himself."

The patient had a to do list—to lose weight. But he first needed a *due to* link—to be healthy. He needed to yearn for a healthy lifestyle and commit to it by aggressively and deliberately spinning his Wheel of Personal Fortune. He needed to focus on an important value in his life—the value of his health.

Remember Yourself

How can you become more effective in spinning your Wheel of Personal Fortune, in creating a personal tension

Wheel of
(Personal)
Fortune

within yourself that compels you to achieve a goal? Write your own obituary!

Imagine you are 85-years-old, and reading the morning newspaper. There on the obituary page you find your name. How would people remember you? What were the major achievements in your lifetime? Reading your own obituary while you are still alive might create just the tension you need to make a few goal changes. That's what happened to Alfred Nobel, known today more for the Nobel Peace prize than for being the inventor of dynamite. His obituary was inadvertently published when a relative of his died. Nobel realized he would be known only for inventing dynamite. He then established new goals and subsequently established the Nobel prizes.

Nobel literally rewrote his obituary. In a way he *write-sized* his life. You can write-size your life, too. You can write your own obituary now to create tension between what you have done so far and what you expect to do in the future. Think of OBIT as an acronym that stands for *Optimum Biographical Information Transfer.*

You can transfer the information about your hopes and dreams—your yearnings—into your life. Begin by writing your best-case obituary as if you had already achieved your yearnings, dreams and aspirations. Then your goal-setting will be more on time, more on track, and so well-linked to your Train of Thought that your goals will be *due,* much like a train is due to arrive at planned destinations at specific times. Your goals will be written, much like a railroad itinerary with specific station stops heading to an ultimate destination. Goals will become things that come *due,* not something *to do.*

Writing down your goals—like mapping out your trip—gives you a greater sense of control over your life, a greater sense of creating your future instead of becoming a victim of it, and a greater sense of WISDOM in achieving your goals. WISDOM is an acronym that stands for the characteristics of successful goal-setting: *Written, Incremental, Specific, Deadline-oriented, Opportunistic and Measurable.*

The two most important points are that goals are incremental and opportunistic. Goals build one upon the other, extending like a rocket and powered with various stages that propel it higher and higher. You can create your own goal-setting rocket to launch your career or business, and other aspects of your life, well above the constraints of gravity. This will help you break through your own self-imposed limitations. Study the following model as you review this example to effective goal-setting.

Rocketing Your Goals

1. Write your *due to* purpose on the first capsule.
   For example: *I want to be healthy so I am not a burden to my children when I am old.*
2. Write your *to do* objective on the second stage.
   For example: *Lose 40 pounds by a specific date.*
3. Write the *to do* task on the third stage.
   For example: *I will exercise 20 minutes every day.*

Like a rocket, your goals are built in stages. You need to ignite your engines with a sense of yearning that stokes fire into a blazing *due to* list, compelling you to break through any barriers. Your booster rockets fill with a sense of hope as your goals launch you towards your full potential.

In this chapter about yearning you learned the power of linking goals to a foundation of values—the power of creating tension to cross your Bridge to Success, the power of more aggressively spinning your Wheel of Personal Fortune, and the power of rocketing your goals with a *due to* thrust that goes beyond a to do list.

Like a rocket, your goals are built in stages. You need to ignite your engines with a sense of yearning that stokes your fire into a blazing *due to* list.

In essence, you've learned to stoke your personal fire. In the next chapter you'll learn how to fuel that fire and convert your yearning into a more purpose-filled passion. You'll then be able to generate a greater lift-off to your career and your life. As a result, you'll get a stronger GRIP on your dream.

ROCKETING
YOUR GOALS

Step: 1   **Step: 2**   **Step: 3**

Value Statement   **Objective & Due Date**   **Specific Task next 3 days**

In Step 1, determine the personal value that you feel passionately about.

Mentally inscribe this value statement on the nose of the rocket.

Example:

Be healthy in my old age so that I am not a burden to my children.

Then think of blasting off in your rocket to reach your goal.

In Step 2, add thrust to your goal by deciding the specific deadline. Then determine the specific weight loss objective.

Example:

Lose 40 pounds by March 1.

In Step 3, add greater thrust to reaching your goal by determining 1 specific thing you can do in the next 3 days to reach your goal.

Example:

Exercise 20 minutes every day.

Chapter 2

Passion

Fueling Your Fire

Passion is the booster rocket that thrusts your goals and dreams into a successful orbit. Take it from the Nobel prize winning physicist who noted that the most successful scientists often are not the most talented, "but the ones impelled by curiosity." Even Albert Einstein admitted, "I have no special gift. I am only passionately curious."

Are you impelled by curiosity? Are you passionately curious? Are you impelling your passion to achieve more of your goals? In this chapter you'll learn how the power of passion can drive you to achieve your goals.

With passion comes our MO (modus operandi) for success—an MO that author W. Clement Stone called a Magnificent Obsession. What's your MO? What are you magnificently obsessed about?

Ray Kroc, the founder of the McDonald's fast food chain, was obsessed with a French fry. "The French fry has become almost sacred for me. Its preparation is a ritual to be followed religiously," Kroc said.

Likewise, George Washington Carver was obsessed with the peanut. He invented more than 300 different uses for it, saying that his success stemmed from his "love of the peanut."

With passion, both Kroc and Carver got a GRIP on their dreams. They did not slip and fall into the choppy seas of the unknown. Instead they were bathed in courage, awash in conviction, and showered in commitment.

With passion, they heightened their vision, invigorated their involvement, and validated their existence. They energized themselves and others. They fostered vitality and a vigor that embodied, embraced, and espoused a yearning. And they turned that *yearning* into *earnings* for themselves and countless others.

As passionate goal-setters, they knew there was a big difference between people who show their passion and people who have a passion for show. The following sign found at a dog show demonstrates the difference:

> *There are dog people,*
> *and then*
> *there are people*
> *who own dogs.*

Passionate goal-setters and dream achievers are like dog people. They are always passionate about what they do. They *sign in* forever; they don't simply *sign on* for a short time. They take their goals seriously no matter what, no matter where, no matter when. There is no show time—it's all real time.

That's why Wally Amos, the cookie king of Famous Amos, used to assert that he didn't sell cookies. "I *am* the cookie. My personality is part of that cookie." Who are you? What are you passionate about? What is your personality a part of?

Taking it Personally

Passionate goal-setters and dream achievers take their success personally, and they take control. They share the concern of George Washington, the first United States president, who was fearful of over-staffing—of putting too many cooks in the proverbial kitchen, and thereby undermining the importance of each individual. He noted that an activity done well by one person is "worse executed by two persons and scarcely done at all by three or more employed within." Are you hiding behind others in not setting your own goals?

Passionate goal-setters and dream achievers don't form committees. When Charles Lindbergh became the first pilot to fly solo across the Atlantic Ocean, a business executive smirked, "It would have been even more remarkable if he had done it with a committee."

Committees often don't commit. In many cases, they spin their wheels in the sands of consensus. They drive to assumptions more than to conclusions. They hide behind each other, expecting the other person to take responsibility. As a result, nothing gets done when something magnificent could have been done by virtually anyone. Consider the following anonymous passage about "Everybody, Somebody, Anybody and Nobody":

> There was an important job to be done and Everybody was sure Somebody would do it. Anybody could have done it. But Nobody did it. Somebody got angry about that because it was Everybody's job. Everybody thought

Anybody would do it. Nobody thought Somebody wouldn't do it. But Everybody blamed Somebody when Nobody did what Anybody could have.

Be Somebody. Don't let Anybody or Everybody try to make you a Nobody. Take control of your goals. Stand out from the crowd. Wear your BVDs in public. Your BVDs are who you are underneath it all—your *Beliefs, Values and Discipline.*

Belief Fuels Your Passion

Belief is critical for passionate goal-setters and dream achievers. With belief comes an overwhelming passion and purpose. And a belief, fueled by your own passion, expands your values and ultimately ruptures your comfort zone, which brings about discipline. With discipline, you have the desire to stick with your goals and stay on the "goal-den" path toward continuous improvement—even if that path takes you through many turns in the road and many different iterations.

Leonardo da Vinci wore his BVDs in public. He parlayed his passion for art through at least three other versions of his Mona Lisa. X-rays of his masterpiece show three different iterations underneath his final painting. How many times have you restarted a project, a dream, or a goal? That's okay. Just keep going—keep parlaying your passion.

Poet Thomas Gray wore his BVDs in public. He parlayed his passion enough to write 75 different drafts of "Eulogy Written in a Country Churchyard." How many drafts did you write when developing your OBIT in the previous chapter?

Author Ernest Hemingway wore his BVDs in public. He parlayed his passion enough to rewrite the last paragraph of "A Farewell to Arms" 44 times. How many times did you rewrite just one of *your* goals?

Wearing your

BVDs

In public

Beliefs

Values

Disciplines

Architect William Lamb wore his BVDs in public. He parlayed his passion enough to develop 16 different building plans before gaining approval to build The Empire State Building. How many times did you review your dreams before settling on your goal-setting plan?

Sculptor Auguste Bartholdi wore his BVDs in public. He parlayed his passion enough to develop nine different models before deciding on the final form of the Statue of Liberty. How many different versions of your goal-setting plan did you develop to get a GRIP on your dream?

Discipline

Passionate goal-setters and dream achievers keep fueling their fires, no matter how burned out they are. Cyrus Field came out of a comfortable retirement and struggled through five failures before successfully laying the first transatlantic cable a year after the Civil War ended. Have you already retired even though you still go to work every day? Are you too comfortable in your "retirement" to really strive for a goal?

Author Orison Swett Marden published a best-selling book one year after his only copy of the 5,000-page manuscript was lost in a fire. He rewrote the entire book from memory! What would you do if your life's work, or at least a major project, were lost in a fire?

Richard Byrd, the first pilot to reach the South Pole, parlayed his passion to achieve his dream of becoming a famous aviator and explorer, even though the first two times he ever soloed as a pilot he crash landed. What would you do if your first "goal-den" flight crashed?

Food scientist Gail Borden focused his passion on inventing condensed milk, even though the patent office turned down his claim three times before finally approving it. His tombstone reads: "I tried and failed. I tried again and again and succeeded." What would you do if you failed to reach your goal three consecutive times?

Beat the Odds

Passionate goal-setters don't give up, no matter how far behind they think they are. Imagine your football team is 32 points behind with less than half the game remaining. Keep hope alive. That's what the Buffalo Bills did in January 1992. They engineered the greatest comeback in the National Football League's then near 70-year history. The Buffalo Bills scored four touchdowns in seven minutes and rallied for 35 points, turning a 35-3 deficit into a 41-38 victory in overtime against the Houston Oilers. They kept hope alive. And so can you—no matter how far behind you think you are.

> ## They kept hope alive.
> ## And so can you, no matter how
> ## far behind you think you are.

Imagine losing a regular season football game by four points. Then, three weeks later, you beat the same team by a whopping 73 points to win the National Football League Championship. That's what the Chicago Bears did in 1940, winning the championship game 73-0 after losing the regular season game to the Washington Redskins (7-3). They kept hope alive. And so can you, no matter how far behind you think you are.

Imagine you are a 41-year-old professional baseball player struggling through your worst season, just one year after you won the American League Batting Championship for the sixth time. You are benched for the first time in a 19-year career. You go hitless in your first 21 at bats. You settle for a miserable .254 season batting average after hitting .328 the previous season. *Keep hope alive.* In your first at bat the following season you slam a 500-foot home run and hit .316 for the season. That's what Ted Williams did. He kept hope alive. And so can you, no matter how far behind you think you are.

Imagine losing 20 straight basketball games to the same team on their court. Then imagine beating that same team three straight games, on their home court no less, to win the championship. That's what the Detroit Pistons did to win the NBA championship in Portland. Detroit became the first team in 37 years to win three straight games on the road. They kept hope alive. And so can you, no matter how far behind you think you are.

Imagine going from worst to first in a single year. In 1990, the Atlanta Braves finished dead last in the National League yet won the World Series the following year. The Braves did it the hard way—losing the first two games then winning three in a row. They kept hope alive. And so can you no matter how far behind you think you are.

Fortitude Pays

Passionate goal-setters keep fueling their fires, no matter how long it takes them to accomplish a goal. Sarah Joseph Hale, a magazine editor, maintained her passion for 36 years with editorials and letters to the White House to establish a national Thanksgiving Day. James Watt maintained his passion for 30 years in perfecting his steam engine. Sculptor Lorenzo Ghiberti maintained his passion for 21 years, carving 28 different reliefs into the bronze doors at the Baptistry at Florence.

Composer Johannes Brahms maintained his passion for 20 years before completing his first symphony. Edward Gibbon maintained his passion for 19 years in writing *The Decline and Fall of Roman Empire.* Noah Webster maintained his passion for 18 years in compiling his dictionary. George Stephenson maintained his for 15 years in perfecting his locomotive engine. And Albert Einstein maintained his passion for 14 years before his Theory of Relativity was officially recognized.

How do you keep your passion flowing for that long? You establish a rhythm, which is paramount to all effective goal achievers. This sense of rhythm helps you overcome setbacks that delay your success. It builds a momentum that makes your performance more effective.

One you develop your rhythm, you'll be amazed at your performance. You'll be in the "swing of things" like Fred Astaire was in the 1938 movie *Carefree.* Astaire danced his way onto a terrace and then onto a golf course. Without missing a step, he picked up a golf club and swung rhythmically at 12 golf balls. All 12 balls landed on the green. The film crew was amazed. Fred Astaire had rhythm.

You too can establish a sense of rhythm that will help you get a better GRIP on your dream. With this rhythm method of goal-setting, you can more convincingly stand out from the crowd. You can more proudly wear your BVDs—your *Beliefs, Values,* and *Discipline*—in public.

By implementing this rhythm method of goal-setting, you devise well-conceived ideas rather than face unplanned consequences—no matter how far behind you are, how demanding your responsibilities are, how constrained your time or resources are, or how devastated you are by misfortune.

In this chapter you learned how to fuel the fire of your passions and successfully launch your goals. In the next chapter you'll learn how to harness your yearning, galvanize your passion and nurture your dreams so that you give birth to goals that will continue to grow. You'll discover how your goals can keep you in action, and how to make them come due on a specific due date.

Chapter 3

Conception

Giving Birth To Goals

With a masterful crescendo, the violinist brought the audience to its feet. They applauded the finale of the concert. Then they screamed in horror. The musician smashed his Stradivarius-sounding violin to the ground. He explained to the stunned audience that he had been playing a $20 violin—a cheap instrument he had purchased at a pawnshop.

The well-trained violinist said: "I smashed that $20 violin to prove to you that performance is based on what's inside the person, and not on who made the instrument."

The same is true of effective goal-setting. Goals are born within. No one else can define or align goals for you. Only you can orchestrate your goals from within—like the violinist.

In this chapter you will learn a five-step *GOALS* process, which you can use to orchestrate your goals from within. Consider *GOALS* an acronym for:

♦ **Gestation**
♦ **Observation**
♦ **Activation**
♦ **Legislation**
♦ **Stimulation**

Conceiving your goal begins the same way you conceive a baby in marriage—with passion and responsibility. Your newly conceived goal develops over a defined period of time—a *Gestation* period. Your goal then grows like a baby through a progressive process of *Observation, Activation, Legislation* and *Stimulation.*

Gestation

You have to do more than wishful thinking to achieve a goal. Your goal needs to first develop through a gestation period in which you are pregnant with a thought that consistently grows, moves and begins to kick you into some response. And like all pregnancies—all gestation periods—this pregnant idea has a due date. Goals are DATE driven. You take *Determined Action Timed Emphatically* to accomplish your goals. And as a result of taking *Determined Action Timed Emphatically,* deadlines become lifelines.

Otto Frederick Rohwedder's deadline became his lifeline—and his life. When Rohwedder was 35, he suffered pneumonia. His doctor told him he had only a year to live. The St. Joseph, Missouri jeweler then began working earnestly on a project he had started three years earlier: inventing a commercial bread slicer. Finally 13 years later in 1928, he succeeded. He not only achieved his invention, but

G ———————— **Gestation**

O ——————— **Observation**

A ———————— **Activation**

L ——————— **Legislation**

S ——————— **Stimulation**

he also lived a dozen years longer than he was supposed to live. In fact, he ultimately enjoyed an 80-year life span, living 44 years longer than his doctor thought he would.

Ted Williams turned his self-imposed deadline into a lifeline that helped him become a legend in professional baseball. Williams did not get a hit the first 10 times he went to bat in the major leagues. During his third game he kept saying to himself: "This is my last day in the Big Leagues." He challenged himself to break his hitless streak and went on to become professional baseball's last .400 hitter, a record unmatched in more than half a century.

Deadlines *are* lifelines. When the National Basketball Association first ruled that a team had to shoot the ball toward the goal (the basket) within 24 seconds of gaining possession, total team scoring average zoomed to 93.1 points per game vs. 79.5. Install your own 24-second shot clock in your life and increase your performance.

Observation

The second step in the *G-O-A-L-S* process, observation, involves giving your dream a deadline—or a lifeline—and making it come alive by what you see around you. Envision your goals. Develop them in living color. Cue yourself like an actor in a future play. Hear the music before you play it. Pop a videotape of *you* into your mind's VCR (video cassette recorder). Hit the *pre-play* switch, not the replay switch, and watch the future in which you are doing exactly what you had imagined.

If your goal is to take a cruise, picture yourself on the ship. If your goal is to start your own independent business, see yourself mentally as the president of your own company. If your goal is to be an Olympic athlete, picture yourself winning the Olympics. Visually focus on having the result you want and you'll be able to figure out what to do to achieve it. Just thinking in words isn't enough—you need to picture what you want. Mental imagery can be prophetic of what you're creating as your new reality. That is, as long as you take appropriate action to back it up, of course.

Thomas Edison was once asked how he accounted for his genius. Edison said: "I never think in words. I think in pictures." Pre-play videos in your mind. Pre-living a future experience mentally is a part of high-powered goal-setting. Your mind isn't able to tell the difference between the mentally fabricated experience and the real thing. It is a storehouse for everything you have pictured, real or unreal, all fears, beliefs, and thoughts.

How powerful is observing? Let's take the example of Col. George Hall, who was a Vietnam prisoner of war for five years. Hall was confined to his small cell every day. Yet within three days of his release, he played golf for the first time in five years. He shot a four-over par, even though he had not touched a golf club in five years. How? He pre-played his golf game every day in his mind while in his cell. Remember, the mind can not tell the difference between the simulated experience and a real one.

Pre-play your goals in your mind.

In 1952, Florence Chadwick attempted to become the first woman to swim the 21-mile Catalina Channel off the coast of California. The day she swam, the fog was so thick she could not see 10 feet in front of her. Sixteen hours after starting her trek, she was pulled from the water—a mere half mile away from her goal. "If I could have seen the land, I know I could have made it," she said. Two months later she did it, beating the men's record by two hours. Even though, once again, dense fog clouded her sight, it did not cloud her *vision*. She clearly saw the goal in her mind and achieved it.

The passion of internal observation is the camera that will put your goals into clear focus. Your vision clears only when you look into your heart. If you look outside, you're asleep. Wake up! Look inside yourself and observe how your mind can help you achieve your goals. Put yourself in a new comfort zone mentally by picturing what's in your heart to do—your dream—and then pursue it until it becomes a part of your outer life.

Albert Schweitzer was imprisoned onboard a ship during World War II. He was confined to a small cabin and forbidden to speak to anyone. But Schweitzer refused to pay attention to his bleak circumstances. Instead, he made a greater connection. Schweitzer used the top of his luggage trunk as an imaginary organ and even pressed imaginary pedals on the floor while imaging Bach's music. Pre-play *your* goals like that!

Basketball players at the University of Chicago demonstrated the power of imagery. While Group A practiced free throw shooting, Group B simply *pictured* themselves free throw shooting. Both groups improved their free throw shooting at the same rate—even though Group B used only the power of imagery. Pre-play *your* goals like that!

Former professional basketball star Bill Russell would sit with his eyes closed watching plays in his own head. "I was in my own private basketball laboratory making mental blueprints for myself," he said. Maybe that's how a San Jose, California man—Fred Newman—once made 88 free throws in a row—blindfolded! Pre-play your goals like that!

Golf pro Jack Nicklaus knew how to pre-play his goals. He pre-played each golf shot before he actually hit the ball. "I never hit a shot without having a very sharp, in focus picture of it in my head. It's like a color movie. First I see the ball where I want it to finish, nice and white and sitting up high on the bright green grass. Then I see the ball going there: its path, trajectory and shape. Then the next scene shows me making the kind of swing that will turn the previous images into reality."

Consider your mind as your own personal movie theater. Keep those goals on your mind's screen with *you* in the staring role. See your name on that house. See yourself as successful in your own independent business. See yourself in that loving relationship. And see it in specific detail so that you can take the guesswork out of your goal-setting. Detail is critical, as Fenwicke Holmes expresses in his poem:

Specify

The man with vague and vagrant hopes
Is always hanging on the ropes
Or vainly sparring with the air
Because he sees what is not there.
He who would build a house must plan.
The kind of house, the height, the span
And know the stuff with which to build
If he would have his dream fulfilled.

And he must know down to the penny
The size of nails, the style, how many
Do you want fir or oak or pine?
You'll have to lay it on the line.
The truth cuts sharper than a knife
To build a home or build a life.
There is one law you must apply.
Choose well your aim and specify.

Activation

After you specify a goal so well that you can observe it—that you can picture it—you are now ready to take the third step in the *G-O-A-L-S* process—*Activation.*

Take action. No matter how awkward you feel, start moving and keep moving. If you feel like you are going to fall, remember it is a lot easier to walk if you are in mid-step rather than just standing there.

Don't worry about where you are heading, just keep moving. You can easily make adjustments to your plan as you move ahead. As Ralph Waldo Emerson said: "The voyage of the best (sailing) ship is a zigzag line of a hundred tacks."

Think of those tacks as many stepping stones. They provide firmer footing to reach your milestones than you may realize. In the middle of the stream you are so engrossed in looking for your next stepping stone that you don't have the time to worry about your present footing. Your sense of immediacy refines your focus. Your sense of urgency compels you to act now.

So, effective goal achieving becomes a series of *activations*—successive moves—on various stepping stones. The stepping stones lead to milestones. And the milestones lead to goal-setting keystones that cause everything to get a grip, much like the keystone in an arch. The keystone is that wedge-shaped piece at the crown that holds the other pieces in place.

Keep moving. Become like Joan of Arc, thrusting your white banner forward against the enemy and then following it. We need to take a trial and error approach in our problem-solving capabilities, like the can-do, will-do mountain climber Jim Collins who noted: "There's a route up, but you have to invent it as you go along." All routes begin with one small step. *A*ction breeds *satisfACTION.*

A four-year old girl's eyes lit up. She couldn't wait to enjoy the iced tea just served to her in a restaurant. But her face quickly faded into a wince when she tasted the cool drink. "Yucky," she said. Her mother intervened: "You have to put sugar in that." The little girl tore open two packets of sugar and methodically poured them into the iced tea, while her mother was busy taking care of two other children. The little girl tasted the iced tea again. "Yucky," she said a second time. The girl's mother looked up and said matter-of-factly, "You need to stir it."

Passionate goal-setters stir their dreams with a frenzy of activity. Action is the first step towards excellence. Passionate goal-setters don't wait for favorable winds to help them get a GRIP on their dream. They embrace the notion of Oliver Wendell Holmes who said: "We must sail sometimes with the wind and sometimes against it, but we must sail." And with that bias for action, passionate goal-setters infuse themselves with knowledge and the capacity to act.

In their capacity to act, passionate goal-setters are like sharks. They know if they stop swimming, they will drown. Since sharks have no way to float without moving, they stay in constant motion. Passionate goal-setters know they have to either keep swimming toward their dreams or sink.

Passionate goal-setters thrive on continuous movement. They know that if they brake, their dreams will stall. That's why the most passionate goal-setters do more than just take action. They *make* action. They know action can bring out great meaning and feeling in their words. They are happy because they sing; they don't sing because they are happy. Passionate goal-setters don't wait for the band to play their song. They dance to their own music.

Passionate goal-setters agree with author Og Mandino, who once said "Action alone is the tinder that ignites the map, the parchment, my dreams, my plans, my goals into a living force. Action is the food and drink that will nourish my success."

Passionate goal-setters are always one step ahead. They know if they don't take action, they could be like a car that develops problems from lack of use. They know how important it is to keep stirring their personal engines so their goals don't become as bitter as that little girl's glass of unstirred tea.

You don't necessarily have to take sweeping steps toward your goals. You can take consistent baby steps instead. In fact, pacing yourself as you move forward is generally better. It's not how far you can go, but how you *can* go far that counts in getting a GRIP on your dream. Always take your goals one step at time, keeping your focus fixed firmly on your dream—your driving force.

In a *Peanuts* comic strip by the late Charles Schulz, Charlie Brown strikes out for the third straight time in the baseball game. Dejected, Charlie collapses on the dugout bench, buries his face in his hands and mutters, "I'll never be a big league ballplayer. All my life I have dreamed about playing in the big leagues." Lucy says: "You're thinking way too far ahead, Charlie Brown. What you need are more immediate goals." Charlie Brown says inquisitively: "Immediate goals?" And Lucy responds: "Yes. Start right now with the next inning. When you go out to pitch, see if you can walk out to the mound—without falling down."

Even if you do fall down in taking the next step, get up again. Keep moving, doing whatever is next to do towards achieving your goal. Before you know it, you'll be ready for the fourth step in the *G-O-A-L-S* process—*Legislation*.

Legislation

When you legislate, you write laws. When you legislate in goal-setting, you write your goal as if it were a law to be enacted and enforced. Casey Stengel, then manager of the

New York Yankees, legislated his goal. He wrote his "laws" for winning the pennant on a restaurant tablecloth!

Stengel was so enthralled with his written plan that he soon saw what he wrote on the tablecloth as his map to get to the World Series. He methodically folded the tablecloth and tucked it in his coat pocket (which I *don't* recommend, by the way!). The waiter noticed Stengel and said, "You can't have that tablecloth." Stengel retorted: "Oh, but I gotta. I just won my first Major League pennant on it." Write makes might. Plans aren't merely something you draw up. Plans draw you in. Investing in the planning process for your goal is investing in yourself and your future.

By writing their goals, passionate goal-setters become more reflective than reflexive, more selfless than selfish, more personable than procedural. Through the handwriting process, passionate goal-setters regularly reflect on their true desires and place their feelings onto the page. They legislate their behavior, and in the process, they add clarity to their goal-setting.

Stimulation

The last step in the five-step *G-O-A-L-S* process involves stimulating the achievement of your goal with imagery. Keep reminding yourself of your goals, whether by a poster you hang on your wall or an artifact (symbol) you display in your office. Say you want to achieve a new level in your profession or independent business. What could represent that for you? A picture of an achievement pin? The number for the volume of business you want to generate posted right in front of you? What else might do it for you?

Decathlon champion Bruce Jenner furnished his living room with a track hurdle to simulate his Olympic goal. F.W. Woolworth rekindled his goal of becoming a conquering leader in the retail field by designing his office as a replica of

Napoleon's study. Even Napoleon flamed his passion with imagery. He kept artifacts of Cagliostro, a famous Italian adventurer, at hand in order to stimulate his sense of adventure. Having a tangible reminder of what you want to accomplish helps you to keep better focused on your ultimate goal.

In this chapter, we have looked at a five-part process to achieve your goals: *Gestation, Observation, Activation, Legislation and Stimulation.* Use this *G-O-A-L-S* process to reach out for *your* "goal-den" opportunity and to enrich your life. With your five-step *G-0-A-L-S* program well integrated and well understood, you can now strengthen your GRIP on your dream.

Congratulations on completing the first step of the four-part *Get a GRIP* process. So far you have yearned by spinning your Personal Wheel of Fortune, determined your *due to* list, discovered how to fuel your fire with a passionate desire, and learned how to conceive your goals so that they come due rather than remain something you are supposed to do.

Now you are ready to move on to Part II of the Get a GRIP process. In this next section you will learn a new way to view risk, and you'll become more aware of your own perception. Let's begin with an innovative look at *Risk-Making* and a redefinition of the whole concept of risk. Then we'll take a look at Perceiving and Perspective.

Chapter 4

Risk-Making

Beyond Your Know-Ledge

Goal-setting without risk is like fishing without bait. It's the bait—the risk—that first attracts the prized catch. Risk takes you beyond what you already know toward something brand new. It helps you gain, sustain and retain your rewards.

In risking—in baiting your hook to fish in new waters—you cast your line beyond your current Know-Ledge and you *make a RISK—Revise your Insight to Stimulate your Knowledge.*

Risk is something you make clearly and consistently. On the other hand, chance is something you take impulsively or instinctively. To passionate goal-setters then, risk is something you *make*—not something you take.

In this chapter, you'll learn strategies you can use to make effective risks and to confidently see failures and mistakes as learning opportunities. By *Revising* your *Insight* and *Stimulating* your *Knowledge,* you get a stronger GRIP on your dream.

When risk making, you delve into new depths of self-discovery. You can go beyond your Know-Ledge and learn so much more about yourself and your situation. Often you come away with a newly found self-confidence, as the philosopher noted in his example of calling to three birds:

"I told the birds to come to the edge of the cliff. 'No, we are afraid,' the birds cried. Finally they came. I pushed. And they flew. Anew." You can fly anew as well.

Make Your Goals *Come Due*

Think of yourself as a professional photographer who always *makes* a picture. Only amateurs *take* pictures. A professional photographer is continually adjusting the F-stops and the shutter speeds to *make* photographs, while most of us are content with snapping whatever we see through the lens and taking our chances. In making effective risks, you need to envision the final picture in your mind. You need to prepare for every angle, learn what you need to do on the go, and make your own way by trial and error.

Charles Lindbergh didn't take a chance when making the first solo flight across the Atlantic Ocean. He thoroughly prepared to *make* his risk with his rigorous attention to detail over every inch of his 229-million inch flight (3,610 miles). His preparation was so comprehensive that Lindbergh designed his cockpit closer to the rear of the airplane than normal. This allowed him to get more accurate compass readings because there was less magnetic interference from the engine. And he also developed better airspeed because of less wind resistance. Lindbergh's customized "back seat" gave him a *Revised Insight* that *Stimulated* his *Knowledge.* As a result, he completed the historic 33.5 hour flight with enough fuel (85 gallons) to fly another 1,040 miles!

RISK

Revise
your

Insight
to

Stimulate
your

Knowledge

Personal leaders like Lindbergh are not risk takers. They are actually risk eliminators! They make strategic decisions based on a larger vision of purpose and passion. They see *making* risks as a springboard to the total concentration necessary to achieve their goal.

Willy Unsoeld, a member of the first American team to climb Mt. Everest, saw risk as a way to expand and enliven the present and release untapped capabilities. He says, "Things slow down. You seem to have more time. You see more. You feel more. And you know more. You are more connected to yourself, to others, to the environment. You tap into skills and strengths that enable you to go far beyond what you thought you were capable of doing."

Inspiring

Risk-making can inspire. Whether you're in the throes of cooking a gourmet dinner or cleaning out the basement, you know the feeling when you embark on a project. You may have only initially planned on grilling a few burgers or just sweeping out the basement. Then once you get out of inertia and get started, you get excited about the project. You get more and more involved. Gradually, as time unfolds and you're engrossed in taking action, the few burgers could become a seven-course dinner. And the basement may get a major renovation! You went way beyond what you thought you were interested in or capable of doing. But you had to take that first step and get into motion. You had to make that first RISK, that *Revised Insight Stimulating* your *Knowledge.* Then you were inspired to do more—to *really* make the risk and upgrade your results.

Exhilarating

Risk-making can exhilarate. Helen Keller said "Life is either a daring adventure or nothing at all." British explorer

George Mallory took the dare. Asked why he wanted to climb Mt. Everest, Mallory said: "Because it's there." And Amelia Earhart left a letter to be opened in the event she died while flying around the world. It read: "Hooray for the last great adventure. I wish I had won. But it was worth it anyway. Her exhilaration stemmed from making a RISK, a *Revised Insight Stimulating* her *Knowledge.*

Rejuvenating

Risk-making can rejuvenate: "(Risk) is good medicine for your mind and body," writes author Robert Kriegel. "Playing it safe can be hazardous to your health. Making risks will enable you to live a more vital, rewarding and fulfilling life." Kriegel also notes that we make the most risks during the first five years of our lives. Coincidentally, during those same five years we learn more and learn faster than we ever will learn throughout our entire life. Indeed, risk-making is a productive process that adds value and fosters greater understanding of who we are.

Stimulating

Risk-making can stimulate. David Miln Smith kayaked 2,000 miles down the Nile River, ran a marathon in the Sahara desert and became the first person to swim *against* the current from Africa to Europe in the Straits of Gibraltar. "There's a purity of purpose that enables me to focus totally on what I'm doing to the exclusion of everything else," said Smith. "I am more able to do things I never thought I could."

In climbing upward on your ladder of success, each SUCCESSive step gives you a broader and bolder insight on your dream. Your revised insight stimulates you to let go of your perceived limitations, expand your horizons, and strive for your goals with a greater vitality, energy and enthusiasm.

SUCCESSive

Steps   To reach your goal

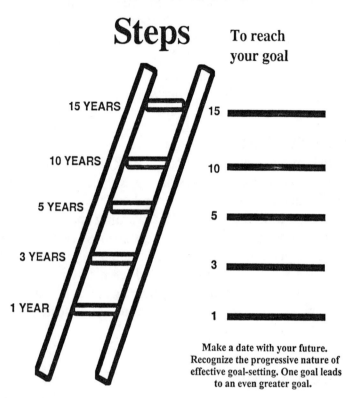

15 YEARS		15
10 YEARS		10
5 YEARS		5
3 YEARS		3
1 YEAR		1

**Make a date with your future.
Recognize the progressive nature of
effective goal-setting. One goal leads
to an even greater goal.**

Elevating

Risk-making can elevate. Ted Williams galvanized his historic feat of becoming the only professional baseball player in the last half century to hit .400 for the season. He could have sat out the last two games and preserved his .400 batting average. If he played and went hitless, he would have lost his claim to fame. He *made* a risk and earned six hits in eight bats on Sunday, September 28, 1941. He ended the season with a sizzling .406 batting average and a firm GRIP on his dream.

Educating

Risk-making can educate. IBM founder Tom Watson called a subordinate into his office who had just made a $10 million mistake. "I suppose you want my resignation," said the embarrassed subordinate. Watson glared at him and then said: "Are you kidding? We just spent $10 million educating you."

What are you doing to *make a risk* in developing your goals? How are you looking at the process in new and different ways? What old ineffective way of goal achieving might you have that you need to replace? Playing it safe? Are you educating yourself for success? How?

Picture this: You are driving southbound. You come upon a road crew paving the northbound lane. A crew member is waving an octagon-shaped red sign. The closer you get, the better you can read the red sign: STOP. As you pass the crew member, you look in your rearview mirror and notice the same sign. However, read from the opposite direction and from a different perspective, the sign isn't red at all. It's yellow: SLOW. It's the same sign but differently aligned. Educate yourself. Make a RISK—a *Revised Insight Stimulating Knowledge*—and be willing to make mistakes—all winners do.

Mistakes

Think of mistakes as "learnings" that often lead to greater earnings. You could also look at a mistake simply as a way of doing things that didn't get you the result you wanted. You learned what *not* to do! And making mistakes can lead to better results. Novelist James Joyce said mistakes are man's "portals of discovery." When you admit making a mistake you are wiser today than you were yesterday.

Think of a mistake as a *miss-take*. A "take" in the movies is the uninterrupted filming of a scene. A "miss" is something off target. So a miss-take—or a mistake—is an off-target "filming" of a scene. And a retake of a scene is simply the result of the director's revised insight.

What do you do if the new scene—the revised insight—is off target? Revise your revised insight! Refocus. Pan the camera and do the take from a different angle. Add more clarity to your *Revised Insight*, which will in turn *Stimulate Knowledge*.

Miss-takes can be pleasantly surprising. Columbus's miss-take resulted in the discovery of America. Alexander Graham Bell's miss-take made him the inventor of the telephone, even though he was trying to invent a hearing aid! Consider these other pleasantly surprising miss-takes if you are ever frustrated with your own:

A fountain-clerk in Atlanta mistakenly added soda water instead of tap water to John S. Pemberton's jar of new syrup—creating Coca Cola.

A factory worker mistakenly left a soap-mixing machine on when he went for lunch. When he returned, he found so much air had been whipped into the soap that it floated. It was named Ivory Soap.

A machine used to press mints together malfunctioned and mistakenly pressed too hard on the mints, forming the tiny candy rings now known as Lifesavers.

A worker mistakenly spilled bran porridge on a hot stove—Wheaties cereal was the result. A chef became angered by a customer who was complaining that the fried potatoes were too cold and too thick. The chef then cut the potatoes into tiny slices and mistakenly fried them to a crisp in boiling oil. Potato chips were born. A candy bar mistakenly melted in a worker's pocket from the microwave signals while engineers at Raytheon experimented with the microwave. This was the happenstance invention of the microwave oven.

A French scientist mistakenly knocked over a glass bottle. It fell six feet to a stone floor. The glass cracked but amazingly did not break. The glass was coated with a transparent chemical that had evaporated—the inception of shatterproof safety glass. Charles Goodyear mistakenly dropped a chunk of sulfur-cured rubber on a hot stove. Instead of melting, the rubber got stronger with the invention of rubber shoes the unexpected outcome.

A lemonade salesman mistakenly left a glass of lemonade with a spoon in it on his windowsill overnight. The lemonade froze and the Popsicle was invented. Scientists were testing a new drug to reduce high blood pressure. One of the unexpected side effects was hair growth. This resulted in the creation of the hair growth enhancer, Rogaine.

No wonder Edward Land, then president of Polaroid, had a plaque in his office that read: "A mistake is an event, the full benefit of which has not yet been turned to your advantage." And Tom Watson, founder of IBM, said: "If you want to succeed, double your failure rate."

Failure

Even though Mark McGwire hit a season high 70 home runs in 1998, he also doubled his failure rate. He struck out 155 times that season, more than twice as often as he hit a home run. In fact, the three previous seasons he hit a total of 149 home runs. He also struck out exactly twice as often— 348 times. So the next time you strike out on the job, in business, or in life, just smile knowing you are one step closer to hitting a home run.

Still need convincing that failure isn't for failures? Here are a few more examples:

Reggie Jackson struck out 661 times, more than any other player in his 21 year professional baseball career; however, he also hit 563 home runs, ranking sixth among top home run hitters. Nolan Ryan lead the Major Leagues in giving up the most walks by a pitcher, before he set the record for pitching the most strikeouts in Major League baseball history. Ricky Henderson set a Major League baseball record for stolen bases. He also set the record for most times thrown out trying to steal bases.

Bob Cousy, one the greatest playmakers in pro basketball history, consistently led the Boston Celtics in assists—and turnovers. Isiah Thomas committed a record 25 turnovers in five games, yet he won the MVP (Most Valuable Player) honors and lead the Detroit Pistons to victory in the National Basketball Association Championship Game in 1990. At the same time, he also averaged 27 points, seven assists and five rebounds a game. And three coaches accounted for nine of 15 Super Bowl victories from 1974 to 1989. But as first year coaches, Tom Landry, Chuck Noll and Bill Walsh also had the worst first-season records of any head coaches in NFL history.

Thomas Edison failed more than 12,000 times to invent the light bulb. Rather than dwell on his failures, Edison said he wasn't discouraged because he had simply learned 12,000 ways that won't work in lighting a bulb! Edison used his frustration as a learning experience. Charles Kettering of General Motors echoed Edison, noting that inventors treat their failures as practice shots. Situations fail. People don't. Failure isn't for failures. Failure is for winners! They literally fail their way to success.

Abraham Lincoln failed to win seven political elections in 22 years before he became President of the United States. At age eight, Albert Einstein could not speak fluently. At age 15 he was expelled from high school. At age 16 he failed an entrance exam to the Federal Institute of Technology in Zurich. Yet at age 26 Albert Einstein developed his Theory of Relativity and unlocked the atomic and space age.

Rowland Hussey Macy founded the Macy's department store in 1858 after failing at seven previous attempts to open a dry goods store. Louis Meyer founded MGM in 1924 from three companies that had failed, including his own. Scrabble, the popular board game, was invented by an unemployed architect and a stockbroker who had failed during the Depression. And Henry Ford built his first car 15 years after he had failed at building a mechanical plow. Ford said: "Failure is not failure, but the opportunity to begin again, more intelligently."

Failure is a commencement, not a finale. It is an opportunity to wipe the slate clean and begin again. As poet John Keats observed: "Failure is, in a sense, the highway to success. Every discovery of what is false leads us to seek earnestly after what is true. And every fresh experience points out some form of error which we shall afterward carefully avoid."

Failure Strengthens Goals

Failure forges champions in the crucible of character and determination. Think of failure as a tuning fork champions use to sharpen their tone and timbre. Only then can they sing their success song on key. Author Truman Capote called failure the "condiment that gives success its flavor." Walter Wriston, former Citicorp chairman, said failure is not a crime, but "failure to learn from failure is." And Abe Lincoln said, "My great concern is not whether you have failed, but whether you are content with your failure." Failure isn't for failures. That's why passionate risk-makers are never content with failure. They are never complacent.

Passionate risk-makers know complacency robs people of their spirit, their drive, their enthusiasm for life. Complacency starves the soul of recognition and reward, of commitment and achievement. Complacency shrouds itself in a blanket of comfort. It strangles initiative and enterprise with its web of apathy and indifference. And complacency imprisons the guilty into a cell of regret and remorse, a cell inexorably locked by the hands of time.   As poet John Greenleaf Whittier ruefully observed: "Of all the sad words of the tongue and pen, the saddest are these: 'It might have been.'"

Complacency starves the soul of recognition and reward, of commitment and achievement. Complacency shrouds itself in a blanket of comfort. It strangles initiative and enterprise with its web of apathy and indifference.

In this chapter we redefined how you may have thought of risk. You learned the difference between taking a chance and making a RISK—*Revising* your *Insight* to *Stimulate* your *Knowledge;* how risk-making can be exhilarating, rejuvenating, stimulating, elevating and educating; how mistakes are only like "miss-takes" in a movie; how some mistakes actually turn out to be highly beneficial; and why failure isn't for failures.

In the next chapter you'll learn how to take more control over the way you perceive the world when getting a stronger GRIP on your dream.

Chapter 5

Perceiving

Shaping Your World

Bloody and bruised, the patient writhed in pain in the hospital emergency room. A medical assistant carefully stitched the laceration on the patient's upper left thigh and then reported he had treated the "upper left cutlet." And why not? He was trained as a chef before becoming Dr. Albert Schweitzer's first native assistant in the African jungle. The medical assistant saw his new world of medicine through his old culinary eyes. Ah, the power of perception.

Perception filters your world—it can blind you to the new and old alike. Perception can lock you in your own mental prison. And perception can make or break your ability to make a RISK.

In this chapter, you'll learn the significance perception plays in your goal-setting and risk-making abilities. You'll also learn three strategies you can use to leverage your power of perception and get a stronger GRIP on your dream.

It's sometimes easy to let your sense of perception lock you into your own mental prison. After all, your perception is your vantage point and comfort zone. The first time Galileo demonstrated his telescope, no one pointed it at the stars! Merchants saw the telescope as a tool to get advanced notice of ships heading for harbor. Hunters saw it as a tool to hunt game. Military leaders saw it as a tool to fight wars.

When opera star Enrico Caruso was asked about baseball's great Babe Ruth, he said he didn't know much about the superstar because he never heard *her* sing. The opera star was also a victim of perception when he met a farmer for the first time. The farmer said he was thrilled to meet the "world traveler Robinson Crusoe." In the 1560s, a French publication sent an artist to Florida to paint scenes of The New World. The artist painted the Indians to look like Europeans. All these people let their perception shape their world.

Engineers at first refused to enter innovative architect Buckminster Fuller's silo home. They looked at the metal walls baking in 100-degree heat. They thought it would be as hot as a furnace inside, especially since there was no air conditioning. But the engineers were amazed when they walked inside and felt how cool it was. In fact, the hotter the sun was outside, the cooler it was inside. Fuller, who created different air pressures to drive out the hot air, had attained something new while others were still ingrained in what they already knew.

No wonder linguistics author S.I. Hayakawa noted: "The meaning of words are not in the words. They are in us." For example, a stockbroker and a journalist have a different perception of the word "quote." A lawyer and a scientist have a different perception of the word "discovery." A biologist and a prison guard have a different perception of the word "cell." A firefighter and an insurance agent have a different perception of the word "risk." We see things not as they are, but as *we* are.

When making a RISK—when *Revising* your *Insights* to *Stimulate* your *Knowledge*—first get a grip on your own reference point. Without a clear reference point, perception pandemonium ensues. For example, a 13-year-old wondered why her parents were refinancing their home. "We still owe a lot of money on the house," the parents told their daughter. "But you've been paying on it for a long time," the girl said. The parents agreed with her. The daughter then retorted, "Well, is *my* room paid for at least?" The daughter saw the house only from her own vantage point.

Perception is so powerful that it affects the way we rationalize and synthesize our world. Norman Rockwell never liked doing portraits because people rarely liked what they saw. Their perception of the portrait did not match their belief of what they looked like. In Leonardo da Vinci's painting of *The Last Supper*, Jesus and his Apostles are seated at a table. However, people didn't eat at a table in Jesus' time. They sat on the floor to eat. Da Vinci accommodated the majority of people who would expect the Last Supper to be served on a table. Are you rationalizing your goals according to what people expect rather than what *you* expect?

Breaking Out of Perception Prison

Are you guarding against rationalizing and synthesizing away your goals and your ability to get a GRIP on your dream? Remember, your perception and interpretation affect you more strongly than the facts and they can significantly influence what you are willing to risk. How do you interpret your world?

Your perception can either be a prison that confines or a prism that refines. As a prism, your perception takes the routines of life and diffuses them into a rainbow of more colorful, diversified, and value-driven opportunities. When making risks to achieve your goals, it's critical that you break out of your perception prison and enter a prism of new understanding, where you can find the silver lining in every cloud.

Ray Meyer, one of the most successful coaches in the history of college basketball, guided DePaul University's team. When his team lost a game during a 29-game winning streak, Meyer said—"Great, now we can concentrate on winning, not on not losing." Break out of any perception prisons that perpetuate the past.

A man working in a china warehouse accidentally broke a $25,000 vase. He was told the cost would be systematically deducted from his paycheck every week. His reaction? "At last a steady job!" Break out of any perception prison that makes you think the world has dealt you a losing hand.

A man suffered premature baldness. Rather than dwell on his misfortune, he said: "Now I will save time and money by not having to shampoo as much or go to the barber, and I won't have to worry about dandruff." Break out of your perception prisons. Maintain a healthy self-respect regardless of signs of aging or other physical or mental challenges you may be experiencing.

When President Herbert Hoover was blamed for the Great Depression, he made a positive connection to the negative attention. Hoover said: "What a great compliment to the energies and capacities of but one man!" Break out of any perception prison that tells you everyone is ridiculing you. Remember this: People are, by and large, too preoccupied with themselves to bother making fun of you and me!

Effective risk-makers hone their perception with a selective power that filters out the glare in their lives and helps them better target their goals. Without this selective power of perception, you could never *make a risk*. You would have too open a mind—a sieve-like mind that keeps nothing in and lets everything out. Samuel Butler cautioned us to shut the mind's doors "or it may be found a little drafty." And William Blake said, "If the doors of perception were cleansed, everything will appear as if it is infinite."

When making more effective risks, we sometimes forget that the door of perception swings both ways: your exit is another's entrance. And sometimes two perceptions can bump in the doorway and create an embarrassing scene, no matter who you are. Just ask former U.S. President George Bush. He was visiting Australia, and as his motorcade passed throngs of people he triumphantly flung his two fingers into the air, waving the familiar American "V for peace" as a gesture of his confidence and support for Australian people. But the Australians were offended and the President was embarrassed. The President pushed the doors of perception open too far. He forgot that the door to his personal perception was now hinged on Australian soil. And in Australia, holding two fingers to form a V is an obscene gesture.

Indeed the doors of perception can slam in your face if you don't factor other people's expectations into your risk-making. For example, you may have launched a new initiative using the successful formula of the past, only to end up frustrated in failure. You did everything right, yet it all went wrong. Why? People's previously imbedded perceptions changed, turning a dream into a nightmare.

Just ask Walt Disney about the power of perception in achieving goals. His movie, *Alice in Wonderland,* bombed even though he patterned it after four previous highly successful movies: *Snow White, Pinocchio, Bambi, and Cinderella.* What happened? The doors of perception locked out the audience. They expected a much different character rendition based on their previously imbedded perception.

They perceived (expected) that Alice would look more like John Tennial's illustration in the popular book of the same title as the bombed movie. The Disney formula, despite its previous success, did not meet with the customers' previously imbedded perceptions—their conditioned expectations.

Previously imbedded perceptions are so powerful they can turn fiction into fact. Jules Verne's 1865 novel, *From the Earth to the Moon*, was so realistic that more than 500 would-be astronauts contacted the publisher to apply for trips to the moon. Once when Verne returned from an afternoon of sailing, people assumed the author of *20,000 Leagues Under the Sea* had just sailed to Africa or India. Another time when Verne was visiting a government official, the receptionist removed a stack of documents from a chair and asked him to sit, saying, "You must be tired from all your travels."

Perception can even turn a false anecdote into an accepted historical fact, regardless of the evidence. History books teach us that Betsy Ross was America's first flag seamstress. But that perception has no historical documentation. The Betsy Ross legend stems solely from a speech her grandson gave nearly 100 years after the supposed personal visit to Betsy from George Washington. The grandson spoke to an influential group, the Historical Society of Pennsylvania, saying he had heard the story directly from his grandmother.

Reputation Tints the Window of Perception

When evaluating making a potential risk, we often place a lot of stock in reputation: how much confidence based on experience we have in ourselves and in others. Reputation is critical in shaping who we are in the eyes of others. Lose your reputation and you lose yourself, as Shakespeare's lost my reputation. I have lost the immortal part of myself and what remains is bestial."

But you can change your reputation. You can change the previously imbedded perceptions others have of you. And you don't have to be locked into one way of viewing yourself or others either. You can use the power of reputation to turn yourself or others around.

For example, you most likely have a store in your area that's more expensive than any other retail location. Because of the high prices, many people may be afraid to set foot inside. If that store wants to attract a larger crowd, it has to turn its reputation around. By simply beginning an advertising campaign claiming to be the "low price leader," that expensive store can give itself a discount store reputation.

Unfortunately, reputation is sometimes too strong, even for the hand of truth to fight. Consider when Galileo proved Aristotle wrong. Galileo discovered that all objects fall to the earth at the same rate regardless of their weight. But the 2,000-year-old reputation of Aristotle blinded scholars to believing the opposite was true: heavier bodies fall faster. Effective risk-makers know reputation can blind you to the truth.

Our Perception Can be Deceptive

Effective risk-makers know from experience that their perceptions can sometimes be deceptive. Mother Nature is filled with such deceptions. For example, much of a blue jay's color is fawn! The mighty but deaf cobra snake responds more to vibrations than the sound of the snake charmer's flute. Monarch butterflies look nice but taste awful to birds, while the tasty Viceroy Butterfly has come to look like the tasteless Monarch—undoubtedly confusing many a bird. And the antlers of male deer look like permanent, powerful fixtures. But they are only temporary ornaments that are shed every year. How might you be deceiving yourself in setting goals and making risks?

Passionate risk-makers know we see *with,* not *through,* our eyes. As poet William Blake noted: "The life's five windows of the soul distort the heavens from pole to pole and teach us to believe a lie when we see with—not through—the eye."

Effective risk-makers know the power of art and poetry to shape their perceptions. For example, the "thumbs down" gesture once meant to kill. That was a perception French artist Jean Leon Gerome gave us in his 1873 painting *Pollice Verso.* His painting showed spectators with their thumbs down demanding the death of a gladiator. However, in ancient Rome, the opposite gesture—thumbs up—also meant to kill. The painting was reproduced and distributed so widely that the perception became the reality.

Paul Revere never made his famous midnight ride. That was a perception Henry Wadsworth Longfellow built through his famous poem. In fact, Paul Revere's ride was cut short—a British patrol forced him to retreat. It was his colleague, Charles Dawes, who did get through to warn of the British attack.

Ben Franklin is often remembered as an old man, thanks in part to Benjamin West's painting entitled *Franklin Drawing Electricity from the Sky.* In fact, Franklin was only 46 when he flew his kite and drew electricity from the sky. Ah, the power of perception.

You don't have to be a victim of perception deception. You can leverage your power of perception and take more control of your ability to set realistic yet challenging goals. Here are three strategies you can use to shape your perceptions and make a more focused risk: Merging, Melding and Mirroring.

Merging

Alfred Lord Tennyson once said he was a part of all he had met. So are you. All your encounters shape your identity. As a merged creation, you are like a snowflake. Free-falling thousands of feet, snowflakes are frozen drops of water that crash into dust particles through a sea of humidity and temperatures changes. Those random encounters make each snowflake unique. Recognize that the apparent randomness (I say "apparent" because everything happens for a reason) in your past, as well as what has become routine, has affected the way you see yourself and your world. Become more aware that the seeming randomness as well as the regularity in your present is affecting the way you see yourself and your future. Acknowledge that merging with the elements around you is a viable method to turn your black and white world into a colorful spectacle.

For example, you perceive the sky as blue because of elements merging in the atmosphere. The sky wouldn't be blue if there were no dust particles in the area. Dust particles absorb much of the sun's red rays, but they scatter the rays of other colors. When those unabsorbed rays merge, they appear blue. So next time you are fretting because of a little dust in your eye, remember that same dust also helps you perceive your world with more beauty and splendor. Urge to merge in leveraging the powers of your perception.

Melding with Others

In knowing others, we can come to better know ourselves. Rather than merge with others, we seek to meld with them— to become a part of their lives, to grow because of them. Mary Carolyn Davis captured this enigma of independence through dependence in her poem, *This is Friendship... "I love you, not only for what you are, but for what I am with you. I love you not for what you have made of yourself, but for what you are making of me."*

Melding into another's perception of you clarifies and verifies your own perception of yourself. My then 12-year old daughter, Amy, was transformed the day a fast-food employee called her "Ma'am." Amy came out of the restaurant with much more than her hamburger and French fries. She came out with a greater sense of personal identity, self-worth and confidence. That brief but meaningful interaction helped her meld a different perception of herself. Meld to weld stronger powers of your own perception.

Mirroring

Think of yourself as a blank tile in the popular board game *Scrabble*. The blank tile earns its identity from the six letters surrounding it. For example, consider the words: FINED and FIEND. Each word has the same letters reconfigured. Now add the blank tile, which is identified as an "R." You have created a new identity: FRIEND. But without surrounding letters such as FIEND, it would have been impossible to create FRIEND. You mirror your environment. You reflect your surroundings. Mirror the magic in leveraging your perceptions.

Nature is filled with a plethora of examples of how we mirror our environment, how we configure our world by looking at the environment around it. Let's take a look into a few of Mother Nature's mirrors to help you gain more control over your perceptions:

In the shade, the sea anemone is always pure white. In the sunlight, the sea anemone turns green, reflecting the algae living in its tissue.

In the dry air, a turquoise stone looks green. In the moist air, a turquoise stone looks blue. In the forests, young deer, mountain lions and bobcats have spotted white coats that blend with the dappled light streaming through the forest canopy.

Under fluorescent lights, a black car in a parking lot looks blue. Under tungsten lights, a blue car in a parking lot looks black. What color are your perceptions? It all depends on where you parked them.

How you figure the world around you is what perception is all about. How you reconfigure the world around you is what perspective is all about. How you integrate your ability to figure and configure the world around you is what success is all about.

In this chapter, you learned the significance your perceptions play in your goal-setting and risk-making abilities. You also found three strategies you can use to leverage your power of perception and get a stronger GRIP on your dream.

Exactly how does your perspective tie in with your perception and help you develop effective goal-setting and risk-making strategies? We'll answer that question in the next chapter.

Chapter 6

Perspective

Reshaping Your World

Bull. Is your life full of a lot of bull? Then take a look at your life from a little different perspective and turn the bull into a tiger. "If only it were that easy," you may be thinking. To the Assyrians it was. The ancient people had a celebrated sculpture: a five-legged animal.

From the front, you could see only two legs, making the sculpture look like a bull getting ready to charge. But from the side, you could see three legs. From that side-view perspective, the sculpture looked like a tiger on the prowl. Put a tiger in your goal-setting tank. Cut out the bull. Broaden your perspective and you broaden your ability to *make* a risk.

In this chapter you will learn how you can parlay your sense of perspective to get a stronger GRIP on your dream.

How you stand on an issue depends on where you sit. If you were sitting in a whaling ship in pursuit of the Great White Whale, you might see the color white as bleakly as did author Herman Melville: "not a color but the absence of all colors . . . a dumb blankness."

If you were sitting as a native in the Hawaiian Islands in the 1700s—far away from iron mills—you would see a visiting ship not as another mode of transportation, but as a flotilla of fish hooks (nails) holding the wooden ship together. If you were sitting as a native in India, you would see snakes as a source of eternal life, shedding their skin in a continuous rejuvenation of life.

If you were sitting as a native in the African Jungle, you would laugh at anyone who tried to tell you fire was deadly. Dr. Albert Schweitzer tried in vain to preach to the natives about fire safety. He warned the natives of potential wildfires and told them stories of whole forests burning down. But the natives laughed it off. After all, they slept with fire in their huts to ward off mosquitoes. In addition, the jungle's high humidity kept fire from spreading.

Where are you sitting in taking a stand on your goals and your risk-making efforts? Are you too close to truly see your goals, to really see the beauty in them?

Perspective is Everything

Picture yourself sitting in the stands at the Indianapolis 500 auto race. What you hear is directly related to where you are. As the cars head around the backside of the track, they scream a high pitched EEEEEEEEEEEEEEE! But as the cars pass you in the bleachers, those same cars no longer scream at you in that high pitched tone. The sound from those engines, which are running at the same revolutions per minute, turns into a baritoned roar that beats your eardrums with *EEEEEEEOOOOOOOOOWWWWWWWW!*

The rpms of the engines didn't change. Your perspective did. That's called the Doppler effect, where the frequency of the sound waves increase as the racecar gets nearer to you, while they decrease as the racecar goes away from you.

Indeed, your world changes as your perspective changes. Perhaps the challenging situation you are facing today can be tamed simply by putting your circumstances into perspective. Things usually aren't as bad as they may seem.

If you live three to five miles north of Big Ben, the 14-ton bell in London, England, and you are planning to go to the park for a picnic, you may be disappointed when you hear it ring because you know it will be raining soon. But if you live three to five miles south of Big Ben, you are delighted when you hear that same sound because you know it will be sunny soon. Same sound—different experiences. The bell sound to the north is carried by low-pressure winds packing rain. The bell sound to the south is carried by high-pressure winds packing plenty of sunshine. What you hear depends on where you are located.

If you look at a burning house, the smoke will appear either red or blue to you depending on where you stand. If the sun is above you and the burning house is downrange, the smoke will look blue. If the sun is downrange and the house is close to you, the smoke will look red.

If you worked four miles *away* from the Federal Building in Honolulu, you would need your umbrella six times more often than if you worked *in the vicinity* of the Federal Building. The Federal Building, which is on the lee side of Oahu, gets an average rainfall of 24 inches per year. Just four miles away on the windward side, the average rainfall is 175 inches. Is it always raining on your goals? If so, change your perspective!

Your Perspective Can Lead to False Assumptions

Effective risk-makers acknowledge that perspective can sometimes generate false assumptions. It can be easy to jump to a wrong conclusion. Consider baseball pitchers Dizzy Dean and his brother Paul Dean. In 1934 the brothers won a combined 49 victories for the St. Louis Cardinals. An opposing team manager asked Dizzy if there were any more Dean brothers. Dizzy replied: "Yes. There's a brother named Elmer in the Texas League." The manager, who wanted to recruit Elmer, later learned Elmer was a peanut vendor in the league! Are you making false assumptions about your goals, about your risks, about your ability to get a GRIP on your dream?

A professional baseball team visited Monterey, Mexico in the 1930s for an exhibition game. Fans screamed with enthusiasm as soon as the team's bus rolled into Monterey. The baseball players were amazed. They had no idea the Mexicans were this excited about baseball. They later found out the fans were in a frenzy because this was the first time they had seen a huge bus in their town. Are you making false assumptions about other people's perspectives?

Norman Rockwell, the famed illustrator for *The Saturday Evening Post*, used to chase dogs to pose in his pictures. Rockwell said many people would jump to the conclusion that he was a dogcatcher or someone who liked to eat dog meat or even someone who liked to harm dogs.

Are you making false assumptions about other people's behavior? Are you asking enough questions rather than jumping to conclusions when faced with behavior you don't like? Or are you rendering harm to your relationship by taking quick offense, based on skimpy evidence?

First-time telephone users jumped to the conclusion that they had to yell into the receiver to be heard. The creators of the first phone books published instructions for users not to yell, even if they were talking to someone miles away. Are you making false assumptions about helpful business building tools that may be available to you? Perhaps a variety of books, tapes, and seminars that could help you build your business or career are just a phone call away. Have you taken advantage of them? They can help you accelerate your success.

Be sure you are seeing with both eyes. Most of us can see almost as much out of one eye as we can out of both eyes. But we need both eyes to broaden our scope of vision and to put things into perspective—to infuse our sight with depth and dimension.

How do you strengthen your sense of perspective and guard against making erroneous assumptions? For example, when you are setting a goal, think of yourself as an actor or actress in a play. If you are making little progress toward your goal, step off the stage. Sit in the audience to get another perspective of the actions you are taking and the results you are getting.

Become like a musician in Gustav Mahler's orchestra. The famed German composer and conductor insisted each of his principal musicians sit in the audience at least once a week. He knew this would give them another perspective of their work and a better understanding of the orchestra's unique selling point.

Similarly, be an astute observer in and of your own life and your progress towards your dream. If you were an outsider noticing someone else doing what you are doing (or not doing!) to reach your goal, what feedback would you give them? Would you suggest they get off their "rusty dusty" and get going? Would you suggest they get a GRIP on their dream, get serious about it and make it happen? Or would you tell them to keep doing what they're doing?

Taking a New Seat

By taking a new seat in the theater of your life, you won't become a victim of your own limited point of view. You won't blindly follow your assumptions and sabotage your own ability to make risks and achieve your goals. You won't end up defeated by your own beliefs the way Montezuma II of Mexico succumbed to Spain's Hernando Cortez. Montezuma believed in a bearded, white god. Because Cortez was white and bearded, Montezuma assumed Cortez was a god and delayed the defense of his empire until it was too late. What unfounded beliefs may be narrowing your perspective in getting a GRIP on your dream?

By taking a new seat in the theater of your life, you open new creative outlets for your goal-setting and risk-making capability. You can turn fright into insight. You can share in the power of perspective that a corporate vice president discovered as she scaled a 60-foot wall in a team-building, rope-climbing challenge. Atop the six-story wall, the challenge didn't look so frightening. "I got a new perspective on the problem facing me and on my ability to solve it. Perspective was the key."

By taking a new seat in the theater of your life, you can turn costly goals into cost-saving opportunities. Imagine you own a successful hotel. Even though business is booming, customers are complaining about the lack of elevators. You call in an architect who designs another elevator shaft for your building. You realize, however, that the entire bank of elevators will have to be shut down for at least a week to create the additional elevator shaft in the building. In solving the problem of too few elevators, you will have to make the crowding problem even worse for a short time.

A janitor, sweeping near the elevator banks, overhears the architect and you talking. The janitor knows that adding the elevator shaft inside the building would generate a lot of dust and dirt on his clean floor. So, the janitor offers them another perspective—build the elevator shaft on the outside of the building. With that perspective from someone outside the architecture profession, the El Cortiz Hotel in San Diego became the first hotel in the world with an outside elevator shaft! Effective goal-setters leverage their perspective. They look at all the angles.

Enlighten Your View

Take a look at a milkweed plant. Under normal conditions you'll see its fluffy cotton balls. But if you were to backlight the plant, the fluffy flowers would give way to a more intricate vision. The light from the reverse angle would reveal the varied vein structure of the plant, bringing into focus a new richness of the milkweed plant. This richness is always present, yet it appears to be absent under normal lighting conditions. Under what lighting conditions are you looking at your goals and making risks? Are you in the shadows or the bright sunshine?

Strive to become like the photographer who lights his or her subjects in new and different ways—to achieve different effects. In the process, the photographer lights his or her way down a newly constructed road to success. The new lighting enlightens. Strive to become like the blind and deaf Helen Keller who saw more with her insight than others could with their sight. She once admonished a sighted friend who complained she saw nothing in particular during a walk in the park. Keller retorted: "I who cannot see find hundreds of things: the delicate symmetry of a leaf, the smooth skin of a silver birch, the rough shaggy bark of pine."

To empower your sense of perspective backlight your goals like this: A father and his son were sitting in their living room. While reading the newspaper, the father came across a full-page picture of the world. He tore the page into a dozen small pieces and gave them to the boy, telling him to put the world back together again. The father figured it would take the boy at least 30 minutes. He was stunned when the boy "conquered" the world in less than five minutes.

The boy backlit the problem by looking on the backside of the newspaper page, which featured a large picture of a man's face. The boy put the map of the world together by focusing his vision elsewhere. Then he turned the page over and the pieces of the world became one globe again. When he got the man together, the world came together. Are you looking at the wrong side of a challenge and balking at making a risk?

To empower your sense of perspective, sidelight your goals. Hannibal looked at his challenge from the side and handed the Romans their most decisive defeat in 216 BC, even though his troops were outnumbered 3-1. Instead of charging the Romans head on, he focused his attention to the sides—to the flanks in the Roman army. He lured the Romans into the center of his troops. He then swung his stronger wings to the sides like gates, forcing the Romans to move so close together that they could not wield their swords. Are you outnumbered by obstacles when trying to make your risks? Attack your goals from the sides. Change your approach.

Spotlighting Your Goals

To empower your sense of perspective, spotlight your goals. When Alexander the Great received a new wild horse as a gift for his 12th birthday, the best trainers were called in to tame the horse. They failed. Finally Alexander decided to tame the horse himself.

The boy quickly spotlighted the problem. He turned the horse around so it was facing the back of the fenced in area, and immediately the horse calmed down enough to be tamed and trained. Alexander the Great realized the horse was bucking not at the training, but at seeing his own shadow on the ground. When the boy turned the horse so that it faced the sun, the horse could no longer see its shadow. Are you afraid of your own shadow as you step out to get a better GRIP on on your dream? Turn around your prospects for success in *making a risk*. Perspective is "everything."

The most effective risk-makers are those who understand that perspective can be *too* powerful at times. It can literally skew our reality, making us "see" or "feel" what's not even there. Consider the employees who complained about the air conditioning being too cold in the restroom. When the blue walls were painted a warmer brown and orange, the employee complaints stopped—even though the room temperature remained the same!

Perspective can definitely alter our reality. Walk into a room painted red and it will look smaller than a room painted blue. Red objects always look nearer than blue objects because the eye bends blue light easier than red. Bright objects always look larger but less weighty. A white sheet of paper against a green wall appears pink. The same white sheet of paper against a rose wall appears blue or greenish.

The human eye looks at a Greek column and sees it tapering at the middle. That's why the Greeks added a bulge at the middle of columns, so our eyes would see the columns as perfectly straight. The Parthenon Building in Athens is another example of skewed perspective. There is no straight line, no vertical line, no horizontal line in the building, yet all lines seem perfectly straight.

By changing your perspective, you can enhance your ability to configure your world. You can revise your insights to stimulate your knowledge and get a better GRIP on your dream. With new perspectives in place, you can block out the light around your world so that you can see the stars in your life.

Perspective is so powerful that we see things with more than our eyes. We see them with our whole being, with our own frame of reference that can either skew or cue our behavior.

There's a scene in the old *Honeymooners* television program where Jackie Gleason and Art Carney are trying to learn how to play golf. They are reading golf instructions from a book. Jackie Gleason says: "It says here you have to step up and address the ball." Art Carney responds, "Oh, I can do that." So, golf club in hand, Art Carney confidently steps up to the teed ball. He stands firmly over the ball, bends over so that he is facing directly down at the ball, and says: "Hello ball."

You can address the goals in your life more effectively than Art Carney addressed the golf ball, when you harness the power of your perspective. But that takes a strong sense of initiating, as we'll see in Part III of the GRIP System.

In this chapter you learned the importance of changing your perspective in order to get a GRIP on your dream and ways to make that perspective shift a reality.

Look up the verb "initiate" and you'll find three definitions—1) to cause or facilitate the beginning of; 2) to instruct in the rudiments or principle of something, to be instructed in some secret knowledge. And 3) to induct into membership by or as if by special rites.

You are about to be initiated in the third step of the GRIP system—an initiation that will further your ability to set your goals and make effective risks.

What is this secret knowledge? It is knowing yourself so you can better shape the world around you, so you can better yearn to earn, so you can more confidently wear your BVDs (Beliefs, Values and Disciplines) in public, and so you can get a better GRIP on your dream. Let's begin Part III of the GRIP system—*Initiating,* which includes Integrity, Individuality and Preparation.

Chapter 7

Integrity

Keeping Your Goals Honest

P hidias, an Athenian sculptor, diligently carved the back of a statue that virtually no one would ever see. He carefully shaped each strand of Athena's hair, even though the back of her head would be situated out of sight, against a wall, and 100 feet off the ground.

A bystander chided Phidias for working so hard on detailing the back of the statue. "Who would know?" the bystander asked. Phidias said, "I will know." Effective goal-setters set goals for themselves, not others. They seek to express themselves, not impress others.

In this chapter we will look at examples of integrity that will stimulate your goal-setting and risk-making effectiveness. These examples will help you enhance your own conviction and confidence in getting a GRIP on your dream.

With integrity, your goal-setting capacity is fortified, magnified and ultimately verified. It is fortified because integrity disciplines the decision-making process; it is magnified because integrity stimulates ethical behavior; and it is verified because integrity more truly affirms and confirms individuality.

Maybe that's why advertising executive David Herbrum wrote that he was less than satisfied with a dirty car he had once rented. Herbrum happened to be the advertising copywriter for the account of the car rental company from which he had rented the vehicle. He maintained his integrity by writing the following copy for an advertisement. The car rental company maintained their integrity when they chose to run the ad. It said:

> **"I write...ads for a living but that doesn't make me a paid liar. If____ can't live up to its advertising, they can get themselves a new person."**

Integrity fortifies the decision-making process. It also stimulates ethical behavior because there's less of a personal struggle in balancing risk and rewards. Integrity helps you grapple with your conscience. Pundit H.L. Mencken called that ethical personal tug-of-war an "inner voice which warns us that someone may be looking."

Integrity, therefore, simplifies goal-setting behavior because it gives us only one course of action—the ethical course. There is a single focus on realizing the opportunity, not rationalizing any obstacles. With integrity, there is no need to rationalize — no need to lie to yourself or others. You are consistent. Your behavior reflects your values. After all, you can't perform consistently in a manner that is inconsistent with the way you are.

We all have an internal compass that keeps us pointed to *truth* north, as ABC-TV news commentator Ted Koppel observed, "There's harmony and inner peace to be found in following a moral compass that points in the same direction, regardless of fashion or trend." Are you following your compass heading? If not, how come?

Teddy Roosevelt followed his compass faithfully. He fired a ranch-hand when he found the man branding an unmarked steer from Roosevelt's neighbor's land. The ranch-hand justified his deed by saying he wanted to please his boss. Infuriated, Roosevelt said: "A man who will steal for me will steal from me."

Abraham Lincoln consistently followed his compass. He demonstrated his Presidential timbre, even as a 24-year-old postmaster in New Salem, Illinois. The post office closed and it was several years later before an agent from the postal service came to close the financial books. Lincoln was then a struggling lawyer. The agent told Lincoln that $17 (or a third of his annual salary) was owed to the post office. Lincoln nodded. He walked over to an old trunk, took out a yellowed cotton rag, unraveled the string and spread the cloth on a table. There was the $17—the equivalent of $10,000 for someone earning $30,000 in today's dollars—untouched. Lincoln said, "I never use any man's money but by own."

Lowell Elliott diligently followed his compass. He found $500,000 in cash on his farm in Peru, Indiana. The farmer promptly turned the money over to the authorities and earned a spot in the Guinness Book of Records for the largest amount of money ever returned to its rightful owner. Indeed, integrity clarifies goal-setting.

A philosopher and author once asked a Russian peasant what he would do if he knew the world would end tomorrow. The peasant replied, "I would plow." He would plow just like he did every day because he believed in living every day as if it were his last.

Integrity more clearly defines your identity regardless of external social, political or economic forces. Integrity helps people more clearly understand themselves. As author John R. Diekman wrote: "The person who is moving in the direction of effectiveness is tuned into his own self. He is in touch with what his insides are telling him. If he is feeling something in the pit of his stomach he knows about it in his head. He is aware of the whole of his inner life—what he is feeling, what he is thinking and what he is wanting."

Louis B. Mayer, the Hollywood movie executive, was in tune with himself and his integrity when he cut short his visit with President Franklin D. Roosevelt at the White House. Mayer took out his wristwatch, placed it on the President's desk and said to FDR: "Mr. President, I'm told that when anyone spends 18 minutes with you, you have him or her in your pocket." Exactly 17 minutes later, Mayer got up, said goodbye and left. Are you undermining your integrity by associating with some people too long?

Integrity more significantly distinguishes individuality, whether you take advice from Marcus Aurelius to "Be thyself" or from Socrates to "Know thyself" or from Shakespeare "To thine own self be true." Actress Marlene Dietrich once asked a Paris clothier to redo the lining in a jacket seven times before she found it acceptable. The manager wanted to know why the actress was being such a perfectionist, especially since the audience would not be looking at a pleat in her jacket. Dietrich responded: "In 20 years, if my daughter should supervise a reshowing of my films, she would notice the pleat and think Mother had lost her touch."

With integrity, you won't lose your touch. With integrity comes a high degree of sincerity and attention to detail in setting and achieving your goals. With integrity and sincerity, we not only design our lives, but we also detail them very carefully.

We can become like sculptor Alexander Calder. He designed a 43-foot high stabile (a stationary mobile) that marks downtown Grand Rapids, Michigan. He also detailed it, creating each of the 1,561 bolts in his 42-ton artistry. With integrity we can see our goals come alive in "3D"—design, detail and distinction.

Sincerity

With integrity, you will be more sincere and genuine — that's true to yourself — as you set goals and make risks. Sincerity comes from the Latin word *sin cera,* meaning "without wax."

In ancient Rome, *sin cera* was a shopping area where the sculptures for sale were "without wax." Traditionally, artists would cover their sculptures with wax in order to conceal those unwanted nicks and mistakes. Those patrons who wanted sculptures that were complete and that maintained their integrity, would shop at *sin cera.*

Golf legend Bobby Jones maintained his sincerity by penalizing himself a stroke when his ball moved slightly before he addressed it. The penalty forced him into a tie for the U.S. Open Championship, which he then lost in a playoff.

In the 1978 Hall of Fame Classic at Pinehurst, golf pro Tom Kite maintained his sincerity when he penalized himself one stroke for the same miscue as Jones. He finished second, one stroke behind Tom Watson.

And golf pro Babe Didrickson maintained her sincerity by penalizing herself two strokes for playing the wrong ball. She lost that tournament, but not her integrity.

Stability

With integrity, you develop a can-do, will-do sense of achievement toward your goals without bowing to external pressures. You gain the stability of krypton, a rare gas so stable that it will not link or bond with other elements. And like krypton, your environment does not affect you. You remain steady on both easy and challenging days, whether you are feeling up or down. Your integrity and stability give you a sense of predictability that others can depend on and measure themselves against.

Like the characteristics of krypton, integrity in setting goals is inherent more than inherited. It can't be given to you—it *is* you. That's why one of the former rulers of Russia, assigned himself the lowest rank in the army at age 13, even though he could have made himself commander in chief. He had the integrity to earn his rank, not command it. He slept, ate and worked with the other soldiers. When he toured Europe as the first such leader to leave his country, he toured as a common soldier.

With integrity you have the power to earn respect—despite your education or experience. For example Abraham Flexner, who revolutionized American medical education, was not a doctor. In fact, he had no medical background. What he did have was "a razor edge mind, fierce integrity and limitless courage," according to author John Gardner.

Once ingrained in your goal-setting, integrity is never lost, no matter how much time or fame or fortune tries to mask that completeness, wholeness and consistency. Harry Warner's integrity—his conception of himself as an individual—was never masked, no matter how rich and famous he became as one of the four Warner Brothers of movie production fame. He often would walk down a studio street, picking up nails and popping them in his mouth. As a boy he was a shoemaker and would scavenge for nails to fix shoes. He never forgot his background as a component of his individuality.

With integrity, you develop a great sense of personal responsibility that compels you to look into the mirror "that no stone can crack," as Henry David Thoreau referred to Walden Pond. Certainly Grover Cleveland didn't crack his mirror of integrity, even though he had more than 400 stones thrown at it during his first four years as president of the United States. During that time Cleveland issued 413 vetoes—more than twice as many vetoes as all 21 previous presidents combined. President Cleveland meant it when he said his goal was to guard against the corruption of pork-barreling. His sense of personal integrity was so evident that newspaper publisher Joseph Pulitzer cited four reasons for endorsing the Cleveland presidential campaign: 1. He is an honest man. 2. He is an honest man. 3. He is an honest man. 4. He is an honest man.

With integrity, an effective goal-setter will be even more poised—not posed—for success. The one-letter difference in those words—"poise" and "pose"—is significant, because the "I" stands for Integrity—the integrity to stand behind your own work. The ancient Romans knew all about standing behind their work. Back then, engineers were expected to stand beneath an arch they had just built when the scaffolding was removed. Are you willing to stand behind and beneath absolutely everything you do?

With integrity comes a passion of purpose, which gives birth to more effective goal-setting and more meaningful risk-making. That integrity boosts self-confidence, spawning what Ralph Waldo Emerson called an "eloquent man . . . inwardly drunk with a certain belief." Daniel Webster agreed that eloquence springs from the integrity of heart and soul more than the conviction in the voice. He said: "True eloquence does not consist in speech. Words and phrases may be marshaled in every way, but they cannot compass (achieve) it.

It must consist in the man, in the subject and in the occasion. It comes, if at all, like the outbreaking of a fountain from earth or the bursting forth of volcanic fires with spontaneous, original native force." That native force is integrity.

With integrity comes a sense of honor. Sam Houston, who saved Texas from Mexico's Santa Ana, wore a gold ring with the word "Honor" engraved inside. Houston's integrity inspired a victory at the Battle of San Jacinto, where Houston's troops killed over 1,300 Mexicans while suffering only 30 casualties. Houston, inspiring his troops with his "Remember the Alamo" battle cry, battled back from the Alamo loss that saw thousands of Mexicans kill 200 Texans.

Responsibility

With integrity comes a sense of duty. John Adams, the second president of the United States, witnessed what is known today as the Boston Massacre. On March 5, 1770, British soldiers, who were pushed back by a hostile crowd, killed five colonists in a riot. All of Boston was outraged. No attorney wanted to defend those British in a court of law. But due to his strong sense of duty, Adams could not deny his integrity to justice as an attorney. He did what he believed was the right thing to do. He defended the British soldiers and won the case, upholding the integrity of the law against riots and unlawful assemblies.

With integrity comes a sense of responsibility. For example, birds instinctively will fly away from danger—unless the danger threatens their young. Then with integrity, the bird will activate its "response-ability"—its ability to respond. The protective bird will use its wings to cover the nest or will pose as a decoy away from the nest. With integrity we respond to situations with a sense of commitment to a greater cause, regardless of the extenuating circumstances. We become like the Washington, DC police officer who pulled over a speeder on "M" Street. The speeder was President Ulysses S. Grant. The officer was embarrassed, but the integrity of Grant comforted the officer. He reminded the officer that he had a responsibility to do his job. The officer impounded Grant's horse and buggy and forced the President and Civil War hero to walk.

With integrity, we behave consistently responsibly, just like the wool fibers that maintain a natural cork screw shape. We can straighten them out with a gentle pull, but they will always spring back again to their natural shape. That's why very wrinkled wool clothing can always be smoothed out. The fibers have structural integrity.

With the sense of duty that comes with integrity, there is no quandary on seemingly ambivalent issues. There's commitment to truth. For example, are zebras black with white stripes or white with black stripes? With integrity well defined, there is no confusion. There is only clarity and simplicity. Zebras are white with black stripes. Why? Because of the integrity in the white stripes. The white stripes are always uniform in intensity, but the black stripes vary in color.

Without integrity and the responsibility for follow-through that comes with it, there is manipulation at best and exploitation at worst. There are hidden agendas coloring every action. Goals are set but hardly achieved, often as a clever politically popular cover-up for what will actually be done. Goal-setters and risk-makers without integrity attempt to rationalize—if not undermine in whole or part—their true character. They may achieve the goal, but at what cost? What principle was sacrificed?

Think about your own sense of integrity as you set your goals and make your risks. Do you mean what you say and say what you really mean? Without integrity we can easily mask our true intentions. We can be like the female firefly that mimics the sexual signals of another kind of firefly. She lures unsuspecting males and then devours them. Or we can be like the song of Lorelei in the German Legend who slayed more than soothed unsuspecting sailors. Or we can be like the Sand People in the movie *Star Wars* who walked in a single file to conceal their numbers. Without integrity, there is confusion and even delusion. As Jesus said according to Matthew 23:27 in the Bible: "You are like whitewashed tombs which outwardly appear beautiful but within they are all full of dead men's bones."

In this chapter we reviewed examples of integrity that stimulate goal-setting and risk-making effectiveness. These examples will help you enhance your own conviction and confidence to get a GRIP on your dream. Remember that with integrity there is no confusion. There is only a fusion of heart and soul, body and mind, thought and action. Integrity endears and endures; it fortifies and clarifies; and it verifies and magnifies individuality—a critical element in effective goal-setting—as we'll expand on in the next chapter.

Chapter 8

Individuality

Seeing I to I

You-nique. You are unique. Only you can be you. None of the six billion other humans on this earth can be uniquely you. Only you can set goals and make risks that are uniquely aligned with your values, passions, and integrity. Only you can be you. No one else can be you.

In this chapter you'll learn to more fully utilize your you-niqueness in your goal-setting and risk-making.

You don't need a branding iron to define who you are or whom you belong to. You can be unbranded. You can stand out from the rest of the herd. You can be a maverick. You can be heard, not herded. How? Be you-nique.

Too often people's you-niqueness is blended (and "bland-ed") away in a blender that whips away individual differences and personal perspective. Goals become depersonalized, without passion, without integrity and without individuality. Goals become branded into conformity, blunted into ambiguity or blended into anonymity.

Branded, blunted and blended together, goals lose their individual orientation. As a result, you may forget who YOU are. You may forget your you-niqueness. No longer can you differentiate the vigor, the vitality and the zest in your *personal* taste. You become much like the honey from various individual flowers that are blended together into a sweet concoction that dilutes your true individual taste. If you were the honey from a lime tree, you would no longer taste like mint. If you were the honey from wild clematis, you would no longer taste like butterscotch. If you were the honey from sweet clover, you would no longer taste like cinnamon. And if you were the honey from a hawthorn tree, you would no longer taste like nuts. Blended bland, we taste none of that you-niqueness.

Have you been too quick to blend away differences in yourself and others? Have you forgotten the experiment you may have done in elementary physics, where a violin bow is drawn along the edge of a glass plate? The vibration moves the grains of sand in the glass to form various patterns. The sand patterns are never the same, even when the same person draws the same bow over the same glass. That's how you-nique *you* are!

Reject the "One-Size-Fits-All" Mindset

You *can* have it your way. That's why the most effective goal-setters reject the blending mentality. Effective goal-setters and risk-makers refuse to sleep in the mythical Procrustean bed (a habit or rut into which someone is arbitrarily forced). Such people refuse to conform to the one-size-fits-all mindset. They refuse to be stretched or shrunk to an exact fit.

Individuals who are moving ahead heed the admonition in Jean-Paul Sartre's observation that: "We only become what we are by the radical and deep seated refusal of that which others have made for us." The most effective goal-setters subscribe to the independent mindset of poet Robert Frost who noted: "The best things and the best people rise out of their separateness. I am against a homogenized society because I want the cream to rise."

Frost again emphasized the spirit of individuality and independence in his poem *The Road Less Traveled*:

> *"I shall be telling this with a sigh,*
> *Somewhere ages and ages hence: Two*
> *roads diverged in a wood and I—I took*
> *the one less traveled by. And that has*
> *made all the difference."*

That individuality Frost writes about made all the difference to aviator Charles Lindbergh, mountain climber Reinhold Messner and retailer Frank W. Woolworth. They all took the road less traveled. They all recognized the basic law of physics that energy is greatest at its source. And they all flew, climbed or sold their way into the history books. They did it individually, independently, and innovatively.

Lindbergh became the first person to fly individually across the Atlantic. Sixty-six other pilots flew the same course before him, but none flew solo. That individual achievement is why Charles Lindbergh became *Time* magazine's first Man of the Year in 1927.

Messner's individual achievement resulted in him becoming the first individual to climb the 14 highest mountains in the world. His secret? He climbed alone. He defied the tendency to team up. There's safety in numbers, but he pursued his dream as an individual at heights where people with ordinary thinking can live only a few hours.

However, Messner was an extraordinary thinker. He was an individual who defied nature. He was an ordinary person, like all of us, who decided to think and do extraordinary things.

So was Woolworth. He was also someone who defied nature—his own human nature. As the founder of a 1,000-store retailing empire, he could have simply directed the operations through others, like most chief executives. Instead, Woolworth dared to exceed the norm, investing himself by becoming personally involved. He individually inspected his stores. He even shoplifted dozens of items and dumped them from his overcoat onto an embarrassed manager's desk.

When initiating your goals, there's greater potential in *thee* rather than in *three*. As Charles Lindbergh's dad used to say: "One boy is a boy. Two boys are half a boy. Three boys are no boy at all." If you want the team to win the high jump event, you need to find at least one individual who can jump seven feet, not seven who can each jump one foot. The best teams are made up of the best individuals working together—who each understand the you-niqueness of what they personally have to offer. Otherwise, when there's a number of people present, there may be a tendency for conformity rather than initiative. The most effective goal-achievers know there is more creative zeal in individuals than in groups. As former president of Yale University Whitney Griswold noted: "Creative ideas do not spring from groups. They spring from individuals."

Focusing on your own individuality—and therefore on your own goals—is your challenge. Some people manipulate people's attention to protect their privacy, to deflect any sense of intimacy, to defer any sense of responsibility. How about you? Do you find yourself doing that? A famed artist wore an oversized mustache with exaggerated points as a disguise. When asked why, he responded: "People look at it (the mustache) instead of me."

Similarly, once when Joan Crawford, the actress, hosted a Hollywood party, she wore a diamond pasted on her forehead so that nobody would notice the bags under her eyes. Peel off your mask. Celebrate your you-niqueness.

Even Mother Nature celebrates her you-niqueness. Consider pure carbon. In one form it is loosely crystallized and soft enough to be used in pencils as graphite. In another form the same material is compactly crystallized and becomes the hardest of all minerals—diamonds. Are you celebrating your individuality to shape your goals over time? Or are you following the crowd?

Mother Nature is filled with other such examples of splendid uniqueness. Consider the following differences and think how your goals could more fully reflect your you-niqueness.

All spider web shapes are not the same. Some are shaped like circles or spheres. Others are shaped like funnels, bowls or sheets. Tree shapes vary. An apple tree is crooked; a tulip tree is tall and slender; a maple tree is rounded; and a Norway spruce is triangle-shaped. Tree leaf shapes are dissimilar. Leaves from a birch tree and elm tree have "teeth" (sharp edges). Leaves on a beech tree and chestnut tree have even larger teeth. But leaves on a dogwood tree have no teeth. All these examples are different, yet each shows many variations of the same thing. When was the last time you really looked at the individual differences in your goals? Do they reflect what is truly in your heart?

Indeed, Americans celebrate individuality, from John Hancock's giant signature on the Declaration of Independence, to Neil Armstrong's "one giant leap for mankind." Even the English language celebrates individuality, being the only language that uses a capital letter—"I"—to indicate the first personal singular.

Franz Joseph Haydn composed the *Farewell Symphony* to demonstrate the importance of each individual in the orchestra. Haydn scored the symphony so that fewer and fewer musicians are needed as the piece progresses. As each musician finishes playing his or her part, he or she blows a candle out and leaves the stage, one by one, until none is left. What instrument are you playing in the symphony of your life's work? Are you still on the stage with your candle lit?

Individual you-niqueness is so important that each person needs to be heard with the unique pitch of the piccolo—the only instrument you can discern when the entire symphony orchestra is playing at its loudest. Incidentally, the piccolo is also the smallest instrument, proving that greatness does not necessarily have to come from big and mighty ambitions. It's often the little things you do that mean the most. Piccolo power personifies the concept of individuality and the conception of the individual. As Shakespeare wrote: "Who can say more than this rich praise that you alone are you."

Even two people born from the same egg can be different. Identical twins are not totally identical. One twin can be right-handed and the other left-handed. One twin can have a smaller left eye and the other a smaller right eye.

Leonardo da Vinci and Michelangelo Buonarroti were very different personalities. If paired, they would have been in the U.S. TV show *The Odd Couple*. Da Vinci would have played the role of neatnik Felix, the fashion plate, while Michelangelo would have played the role of the beatnik Oscar, the leftover plate.

Mozart and Beethoven were very different personalities. Mozart was very deliberate, very precise and very rhythmic. Beethoven, on the other hand, was very imaginative, very emotional and very imprecise. Even though they both composed some the world's most beautiful music, they were definitely you-nique individuals. Those you-nique people achieved stunning goals *because* of their individuality, *not* in spite of it.

Individuality is critical in weaving a stronger fabric to cloak lives that are often too exposed, too bare, and too vulnerable to outside influences. That's why Vincent Van Gogh always signed his paintings with only his first name. He needed to reaffirm his identity and reinforce the concept of his individuality. After all, his own mother infringed on his individuality. She gave him the same name as a baby she had miscarried, which resulted in Vincent feeling like a substitute baby.

Vincent Van Gogh understood that we need to first stand out for ourselves before we stand up for others. That's why the most famous individuals set very individualized goals that are imaginative and innovative. Author Ernest Vincent Wright established his individuality in 1939 by writing a 50,000 word book—*Gadsby*—without ever using the most popular letter in the English language: the letter *E*. Artist Yves Klein reaffirmed his individuality in 1958 when he had a non-painting show at a gallery. He asserted his individuality by hanging white frames on the wall and labeling them "Non-Painting 30 X 73 cm, 80,000 francs." The show was a hit because the artist didn't sell-out on his individuality.

To assure your own individuality, you need to be willing to ensure the individuality of others. That's why the most successful goal-setters and risk-makers reaffirm the you-niqueness in others. As Dr. M. Scott Peck writes: "Genuine love not only respects the individuality of the other but actually seeks to cultivate it, even at the risk of separation or loss—it is the separation of the partners that enriches the union." Poet Kahlil Gibran underscores that sense of separateness, which defines and strengthens individuals to integrate more fully and more completely together in marriage. He observes in his poem *On Marriage*...

"Sing and dance together and be joyous.
But let each of you be alone, even as the strings of a lute are
alone though they quiver with the same music And stand
together, yet not too near together, for the pillars of the Temple
stand apart and the oak tree and the cypress grow not in each
other's shadow."

In this chapter we covered the importance of being you-nique and how to fully utilize your you-niqueness in your goal-setting and risk-making. Now you need to stand as an individual—see yourself I-to-I—and you will be able to set goals that reflect your values, passion and integrity, with a strong sense of personal mission and conviction.

Express your individuality by setting and achieving your goals with a well-integrated, you-niquely oriented sense of preparation—one that goes beyond planning, as we'll discuss in the next chapter.

Chapter **9**

Preparation

Beyond Planning

You can't plan for everything but you can prepare for virtually anything in getting a GRIP on your dream. To prepare you have to prePARE. You must *pare* the extraneous so that you can better define, refine, and align the significant.

In this chapter, we'll look at seven strategies you can use to prePARE your goals. These strategies will help you energize your goal-setting and risk-making abilities so you can convert your dreams into reality.

To help you remember these seven strategies, just think of the word PREPARE, which could stand for—*Purpose, Reflection, Expectation, Penciling, Anticipation, Reading and Expansion.*

PREPARE

Purpose

Reflection

Expectation

Penciling

Anticipating

Reading

Expansion

Purpose-filled goals engage your Train of Thought and help you stay on track. Such thoughtfully conceived goals maintain the linkage to your objective, strategies and tactics. And purpose-filled goals help you to confidently and consistently get a GRIP on your dream and maintain it as you overcome challenges. Purpose is power. Benjamin Disraeli, the English statesman and famed orator, called the secret of success the "constancy of purpose."

Poet Robert Burns noted: "The purpose of life is a life of purpose." When you know the *why* you'll figure out the *how*. Purpose extends, invigorates, and enriches your life.

Goal-PREPARE-ing Strategy #1

Purpose

Effective goal-setting and risk-making begins with purposeful preparation, much like setting the table for dinner. Architect and author George Nelson always prepared purposefully. As a college sophomore, he would spend 20 minutes before each design class making marks with different pencils on a stack of index cards. He studied the tone, value and texture of the lines he could make with each pencil. Nelson's preparation paid off. His teacher called him a master after he sketched his first assignment!

Are you PREPARE-ing to make your mark on the world?

American artist Grandma Moses prepared purposefully. She always framed her art before laying a single brush stroke to it. "I always thought it was a good idea to build the sty before getting the pig," she said. After framing the masonite board, she would paint the background with three coats of flat white paint. This preparation enhanced the contrast and accented the brilliance of her oil colors.

Are you first painting the background in your goal-setting scenes so you can better see your goals? Are you setting yourself up for success?

Japanese art students prepare purposefully. Art teachers and students usually arrive 30-minutes before class to participate in mixing the paints. Are you mixing the elements of your goals with that kind of proactive thinking? Are you taking that kind of preliminary action to get a better GRIP on your dream?

A University of California study proved that if the purpose is great enough, even death can be postponed. In a 25-year study of 1,288 elderly Chinese women, their death rate dropped 35 percent below the average a week before the Chinese Harvest Festival—an event where elderly Chinese women play a major role. One week after the Festival, the death rate increased 34 percent above the average.

In another study at the Tavistock Institute in England, elderly spouses were found to be three times more likely to have a heart attack within six months of their spouses' deaths, than others were of the same age whose spouses were still alive. Knowing you have someone to live for, beyond yourself, is a powerful motivator.

With purpose, you can be like St. Francis of Assisi, the high-ranking soldier in Italy who was drawn toward the monastery, serving as an inspiration to others. With purpose you can be like the successful New England teacher, Clara Barton, who was drawn toward organizing the American Red Cross.

"Destiny is not a matter of chance. It is a matter of choice," said William Jennings Bryan, American political leader and orator. "It is not a thing to be waited for. It is a thing to be achieved."

Purposeful and purpose-filled goals are defined in the crucible of intense reflection—the second of seven strategies to effectively PREPARE your goals.

Goal-PREPARE-ing Strategy #2

Reflection

Reflecting on your purpose is the foundation of effective goal-setting. You need to first *think* your way toward achieving your goals. Henry Ford once said: "If you think you can or you think you can't, either way you are right." Consider the rookie professional baseball player who wound himself into such a tight ball of nerves that he could hardly swing the bat. Casey Stengel, then manager of the Brooklyn

Dodgers, offered the rookie some advice on relaxing in his major league debut. "Look at Babe Herman. Be like him if you want to be a great hitter. You've got to smile, relax, and be happy. Then the world is yours." The rookie snapped back angrily at Stengel— "Go on," guffawed the rookie, "He ain't happy. He only thinks he is." Exactly. What's your attitude toward your goal-setting capability? Do you need to change it? If so, how?

The power of thinking in influencing behavior has been well articulated for thousands of years. Here's a sampling: "A man can be as happy as he makes up his mind to be." (Abraham Lincoln) "Change your thoughts and you change your world." (Norman Vincent Peale) "You become what you think about." (Earl Nightengale)

How are you choosing to think about your goals? To trigger that thought process, you need to employ the third step in the seven-part goal-setting process: Expectation.

Goal-PREPARE-ing Strategy #3

Expectation

Why does a person still experience feelings of hunger and satiety even if their stomach is surgically removed? Because the person *expects* those feelings. Why do divers below 150 feet see red fish even though the laws of physics tell us the color red cannot penetrate that deep? Because that's what they *expect* to see. Divers see the color they know the fish to be.

Likewise, why do the most effective goal-setters achieve their goals? Because they expect to. How else could a pianist who was imprisoned for seven years launch a concert tour shortly after he was released, even though his hands didn't touch a piano in more than 2,500 days? He expected it. "I rehearsed every piece note by note in my mind," said Liu Chi Kung.

How were more than 400 people cured from suffering toothaches by crushing a worm between their thumb and forefinger and then touching the affected tooth, even though the worm had no inherent healing effects? They expected it to work. This "miracle" cure was published in 1794, when Rainier Gerbi wrote a paper on the powerful placebo affect.

To better clarify your own expectations, write down your goals. Pencil them in, which is the fourth step in the seven-step process.

Goal-PREPARE-ing Strategy #4

Penciling

A pencil is to writing what a conductor's baton is to music—an orchestration of thought and emotion, and the outward expression of an inner vibration.

In fact, the pencil is an apt metaphor for the goal-setting process. One end of a pencil always comes to a point, while the other end is always ready to erase and revise.

To pencil a goal is to give it a point of direction, a reference point to get from here to there. Writing your goals gives you time to think clearly about them. Write-size yourself with them powerfully and poignantly. That's why author Edward George Earl Bulwer-Lytton noted—"The pen is mightier than the sword."

Writing galvanizes your passion and focuses your purpose to surmount even the most frustrating circumstances and obstacles that could prevent you from achieving your goals.

What would you have done if the only copy of a book you had spent months writing was mistakenly burned in a fireplace, along with all of your notes? If you were Thomas Carlyle—purpose filled and passion instilled—you would have rewritten the entire book from memory. What would you have done if you were locked in prison for 12 years? If you were John Bunyan you would have written *Pilgrim's Progress*. During his 12 years in prison, Bunyan became so focused on his writing (his goal) that he would often fall to his knees and shed tears of joy after seeing his characters come alive from his pen.

What would you have done if you were blind? If you were John Milton you would have written the 12 books of *Paradise Lost* over a 10-year span. You would have been so PREPARED that you would often wake up in the middle of the night and compose more than 100 lines—in your head. Then, in the morning, you would dictate the lines to a family member. That's thinking ahead; that's anticipation, which is the next step in the seven-part PREPARE process.

Goal-PREPARE-ing Strategy #5

Anticipation

Goals by definition are products of anticipation. They are something to which you give advance thought, discussion or treatment. Treat your goals with passion, and you can broaden your sense of vicarious experience. You can reach the goal mentally long before you achieve it physically. Effective goal-setters leverage the power of anticipation.

With anticipation, you can create your reality with little or no resources. You can be like Jack Norworth who wrote the song *Take Me Out to the Ballgame*, even though he wouldn't see his first baseball game until 34 years later!

In 1908, Norworth was riding a train when he saw a billboard advertising the New York Giants baseball team. A half an hour later he had written his song after anticipating the "buy me some peanuts and Cracker Jacks" atmosphere.

With anticipation, you can jump-start your goal-setting effectiveness the way Ted Williams did when he became baseball's only .400 hitter over the last half century, as mentioned earlier.

Not only could Williams consistently hit an 80-mile an hour pitch that gave him less than 2/10ths of a second to see the ball, but he could also anticipate correctly exactly where the ball would meet the bat. To prove it, he once put pine tar on his bat and accurately anticipated the specific spot the ball and bat would meet on five of seven pitches.

With anticipation, you can heighten your ability to visualize succeeding at your goals. You can mentally rehearse the results you want to create. Through picturing it in your mind, you can "preview" yourself taking the desired action. This triggers a more direct and more determined response when you are physically carrying out the action.

But be careful—sometimes if that sense of anticipation is applied in a negative way it can be so strong as to warp your sense of judgment. How many times have you squirmed in the dentist's chair just at the whirring sound of the drill? Some people actually work themselves up so much that they say "ouch" or wince—even when there's virtually no pain! How many times have you reacted to something negative you thought might happen before it actually happened, or perhaps it didn't happen at all? So be careful to picture positive results!

To enhance your ability to think ahead and better anticipate, develop a habit of reading, which is the sixth step in our seven-part process.

Goal-PREPARE-ing Strategy #6

Reading

Reading kindles the embers of your mind and fans the flames of thought. It flares the fire of goal-achieving, creative, energetic, innovative people.

Reading is an essential key to personal, professional, and independent business development. Speaker and author Charlie "Tremendous" Jones has often said, "The only difference between where you are today and where you'll be five years from now depends on the books you read and the people you meet."

When inventor Thomas Edison was 21, he purchased all of Michael Faraday's books on electricity. The first night he brought the books home, he read until dawn. "Tom's brain was on fire with what he read," Edison's roommate recalled.

Ehrich Weiss also stayed up late one night reading a book he had just purchased about a famed French magician. The teenager was so impressed with the magic on those pages that he chose a career as a magician—and a stage name, Harry Houdini—based on the book's hero, Robert Houdin. Reading sparked Ehrich's kindling interest into a bonfire of goal-setting.

Reading also inflamed the passion of another boy who would one day build the first submarine to operate in the open seas. When he was 12 years old, Simon Lake read Jules Verne's novel *Twenty Thousand Leagues Under the Sea*, and he vowed to one day travel under the seas like Captain Nemo. Thirty years later he achieved his goal.

Reading also inspired Admiral Byrd to set a goal and become the first to conquer the North Pole. His goal gained momentum after he read the fictional account of a North Pole expedition in Jules Verne's *The Adventures of Captain Hatteras*.

Former U.S. President Theodore Roosevelt read as many as three books in a single day. And another former U.S. President read eight different newspapers every day before breakfast. Winston Churchill, once Prime Minister of Great Britain, read for 2-3 hours every day not out of habit or duty, but out of a need to curb an insatiable hunger to stay alert. And former U.S. President Abraham Lincoln took a job as postmaster so he could get access to a greater variety of reading materials.

Reading regenerates, renovates and invigorates the goal-setting process. Cicero, the Roman statesman, scholar and orator, once said "A room without books is like a body without a soul." Edward Gibbon, author of *The Rise and Fall of the Roman Empire*, wrote in his memoirs—"My early and invincible love of reading, I would not exchange for the treasures of India." And Aldous Huxley noted that, "Every person who knows how to read has it in his power to magnify himself, to multiply the ways in which he exists, to make his life full, significant and interesting." But to translate those ideas into achievement, you need to seek expansion—the final step in the seven-part process to PREPARE for effective goal-setting.

Goal-PREPARE-ing Strategy #7

Expansion

In expansion, you experiment with new strategies no matter how great the barriers may appear to be. Eventually, you'll have a breakthrough performance in reaching your goal. (If you are an independent business owner connected to a franchise or a network of others, you need to temper what you do keeping in line with their pattern of success. You need to consult with your mentor, leader or corporate supplier first—before you do something new. Keep persisting to get your idea noticed and understood. If you're told it didn't work before, perhaps with a change or two, it could be workable now.)

For more than 30 years, breaking the 4-minute "barrier" in running the mile didn't seem possible. Then in 1954, Roger Bannister did the humanly "impossible"—he ran the mile under 4 minutes! Was that barrier real or imagined? Just one year after Bannister broke the so-called barrier, 37 other runners also broker the 4-minute "barrier" in the one-mile run!

Effective goal-setters expand beyond perceived barriers, creating new opportunities with each expansion. William James, the father of psychology, notes that barriers may be more imagined than real. He said—"What we *do* compared with what we *can do* is like comparing the waves on top of the ocean with the ocean's mighty depths."

In this chapter we learned seven strategies we can use to PREPARE our goals: *Purpose, Reflection, Expectation, Penciling, Anticipation, Reading and Expansion.* We also learned that preparation broadens the boundaries of a plan and sparks a flow of new ideas.

With your preparation anchored firmly around your values, passions, integrity and individuality, you will be ready to persist in achieving your goals. You need to first establish your personal conviction in who you are, and then focus your attention on what you need to do in a timely fashion.

Now you are ready to move into Part IV of the GRIP System: *Persisting,* which includes *Meaning, Focusing and Gripping.*

Chapter 10

MEaning

Script your Starring Role

Oliver Wendall Holmes, the physician, author and father of a U.S. Supreme Court Justice, physically stood only five feet tall. But he stood a lot taller in his own mind and heart, especially when others tried to taunt him about his Lilliputian (extremely small) likeness. When asked how it felt to be looking up to everyone all the time, Dr. Holmes would quickly retort: "I feel like a dime must feel when thrown in with a bunch of nickels—half as big, yet twice as valuable."

You too can double your perceived personal value and your self-confidence to make more effective risks. How? Develop a stronger sense of MEaningfulness and give your life a more MEaningful purpose, no matter how choppy the seas of criticism may be.

Take a lesson from Dr. Holmes. His MEaningfulness fostered a greater sense of self-esteem and personal worth. He knew exactly where he stood regardless of his height, regardless of who he had to "stand up to" or what other challenges came his way. Dr. Holmes personifies the significance of a well-defined sense of MEaning when overcoming perceived shortcomings and making more effective risks.

In this chapter, you will learn how to refine your sense of meaning and how to redefine and strengthen your sense of self-confidence in the face of frustration.

When Walt Disney went bankrupt in 1923, he used the last of his money to buy a first-class, one-way ticket to Los Angeles. He dressed first class, wearing a red bow tie and a spiffy checkered jacket. He only had $50 in his pocket, but he looked like a million dollars. Walt Disney embraced his own MEaning, which energized his actions. Even though his business just failed, he didn't. Walt Disney still had his self-worth. He had MEaning.

Not "woe is me" but "wow is me— I'm worthy of being successful!"

When Julius Caesar was a young lawyer, pirates captured him on the Mediterranean Sea. They demanded a ransom of 20 talents—about $20,000. Caesar, embracing his own MEaningfulness, surprised his captors. He told them he was worth more than the $20,000. He put his own ransom at $50,000! Within 38 days, the $50,000 was raised and Caesar went free. He later returned and had his captors punished. Julius Caesar had self-worth and self-confidence. He had MEaning.

Attitudes can shape your perception of reality—your beliefs. William James once noted, "The greatest discovery of my generation is that human beings can alter their lives by altering their attitudes." Your attitude is critical in relating to yourself and others. If you think you are too short, too uneducated, too inexperienced, too young, too old or something else negative, it will detrimentally affect your attitude—which will affect your success in anything you endeavor to do. Change any "woe is me" attitudes you may have into a "wow is me, I'm worthy of being successful" fortitude. Here are a few examples to fortify your sense of MEaning, no matter what pity party you may like to regularly throw.

Height Insight

So you may think you're too short to achieve your dreams in a taller world? Think again. At 5 feet tall, French engineer Gustave Eiffel wasn't too short to build the 1,061 foot tall Eiffel Tower in Paris. At 5 feet tall, German philosoper Immanuel Kant wasn't too short to stretch out philosophical thinking. At 5 feet tall, English poet John Keats wasn't too short to help us reach deep into our feelings. At 5 feet tall, Napoleon, once Emperor of France, wasn't too short to conquer the world. At 5 feet tall, Sammy Lee, the smallest of the Olympic Divers in London in 1948, wasn't too short to win the gold medal for the United States and become the first two-time gold medal winner at Helsinki in 1952. All of these people had MEaning.

At 5 feet, 3 inches tall, Desmond Tutu wasn't too short to fight apartheid in South Africa. At 5 feet, 4 inches tall, James Madison wasn't too short to become President of the United States. At 5 feet, 4 inches tall, Olympic Marathoner Johnny Hayes wasn't too short to win the gold medal for the United States in 1908. And at 5 feet, 6 inches tall, Benjamin Harrison and Martin Van Buren weren't too short to become presidents of the United States. They all had MEaning.

Education

So do you think you don't have enough formal education to make intelligent risks? If so, think again. Thomas Edison, inventor of the light bulb and holder of more than 1200 patents, started school at age 8. Three months later he walked out of school when his teacher told him his brain was "addled." Edison never even graduated from grade school! Neither did Charles Dickens, the British novelist, Mark Twain, the author and American humorist, or British playwright Noel Coward!

At age 14, Wernher Von Braun, who would build America's first successful rocket 32 years later, flunked both mathematics and physics. Albert Einstein could not get accepted into any college or university, and Winston Churchill never attended college. In fact Churchill, who would one day lead Britain in its finest hour during World War II as Prime Minister, needed three years to get out of the eighth grade!

Walt Disney didn't start school until age 7. He left school after his freshman year in high school. Henry Ford had less than a sixth-grade education. And Robert Kennedy, who went on to be Attorney General of the United States, flunked first grade. In fact, four of the most famous lawyers in the United States never went to law school: Daniel Webster, Abraham Lincoln, John Marshall and Stephen A. Douglas.

Famed wordsmiths George Bernard Shaw, William Butler Yeats and Ben Franklin were poor spellers. So was George Washington, first President of the U.S., who only had a sixth grade education. Peter Jennings, ABC news anchor, dropped out of high school at age 17. More than half of all Fortune 500 company CEOs had "C" averages (generally meaning "fair" performance) in school, 65 percent of all Senators come from the bottom half of their classes, and 50 percent of millionaire entrepreneurs never finished college. All these people had MEaning.

Experience

So do you think your lack of experience is keeping you from making effective risks and achieving your goals? If so, think again. Consider what Plato wrote thousands of years ago: "Experience takes away more than it adds." Charles Lindbergh used his lack of experience to fly his way into the history books. He flew solo across the Atlantic Ocean in a flight that was five times longer than anything he had ever experienced. In his book, *The Spirit of St. Louis*, Lindbergh wrote: "The novice has a poet's eye. He sees and feels where the expert's senses have been callused by experience. Contact tends to dull appreciation. In the detail of the familiar one loses awareness of the strange. First impressions have a clarity of line and color which experience may forget and not regain."

"The novice has a poet's eye.
He sees and feels where
the expert's senses have been
callused by experience."

Experience often comes too late: you take the test first and then learn the lesson. Like the Chinese proverb says: "Experience is a comb that nature gives us when we are bald." Or, as Oscar Wilde noted: "Experience is the name everyone gives to his mistakes."

Sometimes no experience is best, because the perception of an experience can paralyze us in fear, even if the experience itself is not dangerous. Mark Twain noted the experience of the cat that sat down on a hot stove lid: "She will never sit down on a hot stove lid again, and that's well. But," he added, "she will never sit down on a cold one any more either!"

Dynamic Debuts

Sports are filled with stories of novices overcoming experienced competitors to make dynamic debuts. Tiger Woods, at age 21, became the youngest person to win the Masters Golf Championship (by a record 12 strokes in 1997) in a field of players who averaged 15 years older. Bob Mathias won the decathlon in the 1948 Olympics with less than six months of experience. Before that, he had never thrown a javelin. Yet he clinched the gold medal by throwing the javelin 31 feet farther than his nearest competitor.

Quarterback Frank Reich, making only his seventh start in eight NFL seasons, led the Buffalo Bills to the biggest come-from-behind victory in pro football history in the 1992 playoffs. Reich threw four touchdown passes in the second half to turn a 35-3 halftime deficit into a 41-38 victory in overtime against the Houston Oilers.

Jackie Robinson, who broke baseball's color barrier, also broke into the major leagues in a major way. He led the league in hitting and in stolen bases, and he captured Rookie of the Year honors.

Another rookie, Gale Sayers, scored a record 22 touchdowns for the Chicago bears in 1965. Bobo Holloman, in his first major league start, pitched a no-hitter in 1953 for the St. Louis Browns.

In his pitching debut, Babe Ruth tossed a 6-0 shutout and went on to win 65 games in three seasons, including a pair of 23-victory seasons. Jim Abbott debuted in the major leagues in 1989 as a one-armed pitcher for the Los Angeles Angels and won 12 games.

Chuck Tanner, a pro baseball manager, hit a home run the first time he went to bat in the major leagues. Roy Campanella, a Brooklyn Dodger catcher, reached second base the first time he batted in the major leagues. He had a total of three hits in four times at bat in that first game. Then in his second major league baseball game, Campanella collected three hits. One of those hits—a triple—soared so far that he reached third base on one swing of the bat.

Ted Williams broke through the coveted .400 barrier in major league baseball nearly three times faster than any previous hitter. That means he was able to consistently get a hit 4 out of every 10 times at bat. His record for most consistent hitting, set in 1941, still stands. Even more MEaningful, Williams needed only three years experience in the major leagues before he broke the record for most hits in times at bat for a single season. The previous record holder needed eight years of experience in the major leagues before breaking the coveted .400 barrier. All these people had MEaning.

Youth

So do you think you're too young to make effective risks and achieve your dreams? Think again. At age 7, Shirley Temple was the United States' number one box office attraction. At 8, she was on the cover of *Time* magazine. At age 10, Edward VI became King of England in 1547. At age 11, Benedict IX was named Pope. At age 12, Elizabeth Barrett Browning could read Greek and Latin. At age 13, Stevie Wonder became the youngest person to have a number one selling record album in 1963. At age 19, Louis Braille invented a system of dots that would help the blind to read. They all had MEaning.

Age

So you think you are too old to make MEaningful risks and succeed in reaching your goals? Think again. At age 100, Grandma Moses was still painting. At age 98, Dimitrion Yordanidis became the oldest finisher in the 26-mile, 385-yard marathon. At age 92, a chief executive officer of a large company was still at it. At age 91, Eamon de Valera was serving as President of Ireland.

At age 89, Dr. Albert Schweitzer was still performing surgery. At age 89, Dr. Michael DeBakey — inventor of the heart-lung machine's rollerpump—was still doing surgery and working 12-14 hours a day. At age 88, Pablo Casals, the cellist, was still performing in concert. At age 80, George Burns won his first Oscar. What did all these people have in common? They all had MEaning.

In this chapter we learned that regardless of your height, education, experience or age, you can put more MEaning into your sense of *Persisting* to get a GRIP on your dream. The key is to focus on what has the most MEaning to you, as you will learn more about in the next chapter on Focusing.

Chapter *11*

Focusing

Staying the Course

Henry Kaiser waded knee deep into a sea of mud. The ship building company president surveyed the muddled and muddied mess. A flood had swept away a levee and buried Kaiser's bulldozers and other heavy equipment in a quagmire of mud and machinery.

Kaiser's employees were devastated at the loss that turned a would-be shipbuilding yard into a gigantic mud pie. But Kaiser was upbeat and said, "I don't see any mud." One of the employees chided Kaiser, saying, "Just look around. We are buried in mud." Kaiser looked sternly at the employee and retorted, "The difference is this: you are looking down and can't see anything but mud. But I am looking up where I can see nothing but sunshine and a clear blue sky."

In this chapter you will learn how to focus your sense of meaning to rise above, i.e., to go *over* obstacles, not against them. Focusing on the positive helps you to find the "silver lining"—no matter how dark the cloud may appear to be. As you persistently go after your goals, you need to focus on the light (the positive), not on the blight (the negative) in your life.

At age 45, George Foreman focused on the light when he became the oldest person to ever win a heavyweight boxing championship. Foreman did it the hard way: he came from behind late in the fight (10th round), against an opponent 20 years younger. Foreman landed a right hand punch that knocked out Michael Moorer—propelling himself into the heavyweight boxing championship throne room—more than 20 years after losing the heavyweight boxing championship to Muhammad Ali.

Unfortunately, most of us turning 40 concentrate on those "40 winters besieging thy brow," as Shakespeare noted. We focus on the negative images of 40.

When I turned 40, I focused on the more positive "Life begins at Forty" posture. To help me maintain that "forty-fying" focus, I wrote a letter of understanding to myself. That letter developed into an essay of assurance. It helped me persist in getting a GRIP on my dream. I provide that letter here as an example of how you can refocus your thinking and turn the blahs into the ahs!

FORTE!

I'm forty-something—make that *forte*-something. I thought my 40th birthday would wring the last drops of youth out of me like a spent sponge. But I survived, thrived and even found my forte at forty.

I found my forte in a secret passage of sorts, a passage carved out more than 100 years ago in the imagination of author Jules Verne, a passage I had all but forgotten. Then it hit me. The passage from Jules Verne's classic *From the Earth to the Moon* seemed to explode off page 117. It rocketed me into a new world of self-discovery and guided me around the frightful forties and into the fabulous "fortes".

There, the visionary author who saw deep into the heavens, deep into the sea and deep into the center of the earth, helped me see deeper into the center of me There he launched the first manned moon rocket 104 years before Neil Armstrong. But Verne used a count-up rather than a count-down: "... thirty-seven, thirty-eight, thirty-nine, forty. Fire."

That's it!   Now I understood. Forty was the lift off, launching me into a higher self-awareness than ever before in my previous 14,610 days. Now after 40 years of refueling and recharging, I was in for the blast of my life. I was a kid again. I couldn't wait to go outside to explore sandboxes and sandlots of another kind.   Once again I was the excited 7th grade basketball player who couldn't wait to get into the game because I had practiced so long—350,640 hours.

Of course, when I get in the game these days, I realize my dawn is gone. I have entered the noon of my life. I can see the shadows beginning to outline my life. The clock is ticking louder for me. But I'm stimulated more than frustrated. So what if the tape recorder wound into my mind is no longer on fast-forward? I've found the "Play" button. Now I can hear myself better than ever before. I *feel* so much more than I ever have. I laugh more. I cry more. I see *so* much more.

So what if the tape recorder wound into my mind is no longer on fast-forward? I've found the "Play" button.

I know what psychologist Abraham Maslow meant when he said, "As you age everything gets doubly precious and piercingly important." I can no longer be content just looking at flowers. Now I am "stabbed" by the metaphorical flowers in my life. It is a stab that pricks my sensibilities, like a slap that sobers.

Slapped into my new reality, today I focus more on looking into my head and heart, not simply getting ahead for the sake of doing so. I have awakened to a personal declaration of independence: I am free because I am me — and I know better now what I want, and what's important and what isn't. When I look outside, I only dream. But when I look inside, I awake.

I am blasting off into the second half of my life with a sense of clarity, of fusion more than confusion; a coming together (as I get older) of my experience, wisdom, knowledge, and understanding. I won't claim that I know all I am. But I am gaining more stability, much like a sword's forte—the strongest part of the blade. And my perspective is broadening, ever-extending like a sword finally unsheathed.

I am gaining more stability much like a sword's forte—the strongest part of the blade.

I accept my new reality. Of course, "reading between the lines" takes on a new meaning for me every morning—when I look into the mirror. My actions creak louder than my words. "Outta sight"—a favorite expression in my college days—smacks of a grim reality. And I can still see myself in that *Peanuts* comic strip where Charlie Brown says he's worried about his 40-year-old father who sits at the kitchen table eating cold cereal and looking at pictures in his old high school yearbook. I, too, used to see 40 merely as a NUMBer.

But now I see an added dimension to the number, a dimension well beyond *forte*-fying images. It's like Ernie

Nevers scoring a record 40 points in a single pro football game in 1929; like The Beatles performing on the Ed Sullivan show on the 40th day of the year in 1964, or like Americans listening to the Top 40 musical hits. Now I see something extra.

At 40, John Glenn became the first American to orbit the earth. At 40, Florence Nightingale founded a school and home for nurses in London; Dr. Jonas Salk developed a polio vaccine; Ben Franklin first became interested in electricity; Mark Twain wrote *Tom Sawyer*; and Lady Astor became the first woman elected to the British Parliament.

At 41, Christopher Columbus landed in the New World; Julius Caesar earned his first command; Samuel Morse invented the telegraph; Harriet Beecher Stowe wrote *Uncle Tom's Cabin*; and Ernest Hemingway wrote *For Whom the Bell Tolls*.

For me, the Roman numeral for 40 is like an XL label. The XL tags an extra large portion of life for me to savor with *X-L ence*. And oh, what *X-L ence* in the forty-something baseball heroes.

At 40, Hank Aaron broke Babe Ruth's home run hitting record; Ted Williams collected seven hits in his last 11 at bats to win the American League batting title for the second straight year and fourth time in his career; Warren Spahn pitched a no-hitter; and Babe Ruth hit a massive 600-foot home run.

All of us don't have that kind of physical power to wrestle the hands of time. But as a "forte" year old, I am convinced I have a certain personal power. I'm more concentrated on *where I'm going* rather than *who I am*.

Now my personal power is harnessed in a well-tuned engine with 40 years of experience and education. My engine will boost my "fortes" well beyond my forties and will thrust me deeper in the center of my mission in life.

Lift off! Mission Control we have lift off!....Forty-one...forty-two... forty three...

Learning to Focus

Focusing away from the negative and towards the positive is a learned skill. Let's take a lesson in focusing from Sgt. Dexter Rainer, the most experienced guard at the Tomb of the Unknown Soldiers at Arlington National Cemetery in Washington, DC.

For more than nine years, Sgt. Rainer stood at attention for four or five shifts a day—30-minutes a shift. "Lightning could strike the plaza (where he stands at attention) and my focus does not change," said Rainer, then with the 1st Battalion, Third United States Infantry from Fort Myer, Virginia. During each 30-minute shift, he would reinforce his focus every 21 seconds, when he would either have to shift his rifle to the other shoulder or walk the 21 steps to the opposite side of the plaza. Just to keep his mind in focus and retain confidence in his cadence, he counted over and over again—85 times in a 30 minute session—from 1 to 21. He counted consistently, methodically, and persistently, but not absent-mindedly. How often do you recite your goals to yourself, over and over again?

What can you learn from Sgt. Rainer about focusing your thinking so that you can more effectively persist in getting a GRIP on your dream? *Purpose drives your focus.* The stronger your sense of purpose, the stronger your sense of focus. Rainer said that he was always "making a connection of what I am doing to why I am doing it. I keep thinking about all the soldiers who died in war, all of those who paid the price. In some small way I'm giving back to those who fought for the freedom we have today."

Purpose focused Sgt. Rainer's performance. The better you define your purpose, the better you'll refine your performance. But how do you focus more fully on your purpose? Ignore what surrounds you. Ignore all those interruptions that seem to envelop you, interruptions that seem to confine you, interruptions that seem to imprison you. Instead, concentrate on what you've put around your life: your dreams, your aspirations, your hopes. Encircle those dreams *around* you as if they were a blanket on a cold evening. Don't surround yourself with anything and everything and wind up with nothing long-term.

Focus on what's around you, not simply what surrounds you.

People who focus on their long-range important goal, embrace and understand the focus of poet Henry Abbey, who saw in a tree much more than meets the eye. Abbey wrote the following poem in the 19th century, when ships were made from trees. Of course he envisioned something more than a tree:

> *What do we plant whenever we plant a tree?*
> *We plant the ship that will cross the sea.*
> *We plant the mast, which will carry the sails.*
> *We plant the planks to withstand the gales.*

Let's take another lesson in focusing from a former American Trucking Association's National Driver of the Year. Imagine driving three million accident-free miles over 30 years. Behind the wheel for that many miles most of us would get bored or distracted, at the seemingly endless stream of white lines piercing our eyes like arrows, mile after mile after mile. But that's because we may only see the future of the road. Refocus and *you will see the road to the future*. That's what Al Koole sees:

"You can't get bored when you think of why you are doing what you are doing," says Koole. He has driven the equivalent of six trips to the moon and back in delivering office furniture for Steelcase Inc., "I'm always thinking how important it is for me to get this furniture to the customer on time. The customer is relying on me," he notes.

What can we learn from Koole's millions of miles behind the wheel? We can learn how to focus on the new and different in the familiar and the routine. "I have never seen the same thing twice, no matter how many times I've been down the same road," said Koole.

He has driven the same 170-mile route from Grand Rapids, Michigan to or through Chicago more than 2,000 times. He knows every billboard, gas station and traffic light en route. Yet he always *expects* to see something different, and that's the key to focusing—a sense of expectation (as we reviewed in Chapter 9 on Preparation). "It's as if my head is on a swivel. I am looking at the mirrors, looking at the road, looking everywhere, staying alert, thinking of that customer and how important it is that I keep performing to meet my promise. In the process I am focusing my eyes to be ready to see anything new and different," he says.

With that kind of focused attention, you won't be pigeonholed into a small slot in your world, no matter how strong the outside forces may be. Refocus, refocus, refocus. Jackie Robinson didn't see himself as the first black player to play in major league baseball. Only others did! On his first day in a Dodger uniform, Robinson told his wife how she could find him out on the baseball diamond at Ebbets Field. "You won't have any trouble recognizing me," he paused, "My number is 42." Jackie Robinson was focusing on his uniform, not on his color.

An American statesman, Henry Clay didn't see himself as a Southerner—even though he was from Kentucky, at that time a southern slave-holding state. Others unfairly identified him with his birthplace, as if that dictated his attitude toward slavery. Clay courageously fought against slavery, and against his southern label. Clay said: "I know no South, no

North, no East, no West." That phrase is engraved on a 120-foot monument marking Clay's grave in Lexington, KY. Henry Clay was focused on a much bigger picture.

Stevie Wonder doesn't think of himself as blind for life. Others generally do. The singer and musician was asked if he had been blind all his life. Wonder retorted: "Well, not yet." Stevie Wonder is focused on his life, not his blindness.

Targeting Your Focus

How do you refocus, especially when your world keeps reshaping, revolving and readjusting like a kaleidoscope gone wild? You need to be able to selectively narrow your focus. Hank Aaron selectively narrowed his focus well enough to become professional baseball's all-time career home run hitter. While warming up in the on-deck circle, Aaron would take off his baseball cap and stare at the pitcher through one of the small holes on top of the cap. The small holes selectively framed the pitcher's action and just as significantly blocked out extraneous information.

Unfortunately, most of us don't have hats with small holes to help us focus our attention. In fact, most of us seem to be wearing mesh hats, which have hundreds of holes that become like a sieve for information to flow in and out of our attention spans. By wearing these types of hats, we ultimately end up chasing our tails instead of our tale—our story, our dream, our goal. We seem to be riding an endless merry-go-around to nowhere. We are busy being busy.

Are you too busy just being busy?

Author John W. Gardner noted that, "We can keep ourselves so busy, fill our lives with so many diversions, stuff our heads with so much knowledge, involve ourselves with so many people and cover so much ground that we never have time to probe the fearful and wonderful world within." It's no wonder then that some people often feel like those circling caterpillars of French naturalist Jean Henri Fabre. The caterpillars are involved but never truly engaged. They're active but never taking any meaningful action—focusing but never really focused.

Do you sometimes feel manipulated like those caterpillars? They are seemingly paying attention, but without any real intention. They parade around and around a flowerpot for seven days and seven nights. Each caterpillar pays perfection attention to the caterpillar in front of it and blindly marches to its own death. Tragically, the focusing but-never-really-focused caterpillars starve to death, even though food is just inches away. Are your dreams and goals starving for food that is only inches away from you? For example, are there books, tapes and seminars you need to be taking advantage of to build your business or career, that you're ignoring? Or worse yet, are you impulsively drawn into some other activity, one that doesn't support your dreams and goals, without your even thinking about it? Are you like the moth so habitually, so mindlessly drawn into the light that it kills itself in the process? Are you inadvertently killing your dreams and goals, by being too busy doing unrelated things?

Impulsive thinking—unfocused and unfiltered—can veer your life, your job, and your family drastically out of alignment. It can stifle your flexibility and smother your innovation. Impulsive thinking can turn your dreams into nightmares.

Imagine how embarrassed baseball great Lou Gehrig must have felt when he lost his grip to impulsive thinking. In 1931, Gehrig could have won the home-run title in the American league, but he had to settle for a tie with Babe Ruth when he lost his focus during a mid-season game.

Gehrig hit a home run. Then he trotted around the bases with his head down. He did not notice that the base-runner in front of him had veered off the base-path to get a sip of water. Gehrig, who was unfocused and unfiltered, passed the runner. That's a violation of the rules. Therefore, his home run did not count.

How habitual is your behavior?

Earl Morrall's impulsive thinking blinded him to what virtually everyone else in the stadium could plainly see on the football field. His receiver—Jimmy Orr—could have easily caught a touchdown pass from Morrall. Orr was in the endzone—in scoring territory—and there were no opposing players near him. In fact, Orr frantically jumped up and down and waved his hands trying to get Morrall's attention. But Morrall's impulsive thinking prevented him from seeing the obvious and his Baltimore Colts lost the Super Bowl to the New York Jets. Are you missing obvious opportunities to score touchdowns in the game of your life?

Imagine how embarrassed the waitress must have felt when she lost her grip to impulsive thinking. She served a vodka-tonic to a two-year-old whose parents had ordered her Sprite, a clear liquid soda that looks like a vodka-tonic. The restaurant settled out of court with the parents for roughly 5,000 times the cost of a Sprite.

Imagine how embarrassed the funeral home in Houston, Texas must have felt when they lost their grip to impulsive thinking. They put the right clothes on the wrong body. Stay focused to get a GRIP on your dream.

Don't glaze over life mindlessly. Instead, blaze into life mindfully. Turn off your mental "automatic pilot." Stop *overlooking* and start *looking over* the scenery in your life.

Disengage your mental "cruise control" and accelerate your life's goals. The more you cruise through your life, without paying attention, the more you become conditioned to react routinely, rather than being "cognitioned" to respond innovatively.

British soldiers in World War I conditioned themselves to delay the firing of a cannon. Two soldiers habitually came to attention shortly before the cannon was fired. They were doing what they had been trained to do: hold the horses. Of course they no longer used horses to pull the cannon in World War I, but the habitually conditioned soldiers kept the protocol in place. Is that how you want to be? Or are you willing to step outside of the box of your old behaviors so you can move on?

How habitual is *your* behavior? How many times have you put your car key into the wrong car door in a dimly lit parking lot? How many times have you taken clothes to the cleaners, paid for the clothes you were picking up, and then walked out without taking your just-paid-for clothes? How many times have you reached for the ringing alarm on the table even though it's no longer there? How many times have you taken your checkbook to the store, only to discover there were no more checks in it? And of course, how many times have you written the previous year on checks, especially during January?

Turn off your automatic pilot. Take control of your flight to success. Do more than just pay attention to your "flight plan." Really *focus* on it!

What's Your Tendancy—to Simply Pay Attention or to Really Focus?

If you simply pay attention, you would think that Canada is a land of mountains and prairies. But when you really focus, you'll see that Canada is also a land of one million lakes—more lakes than there are on the rest of the earth combined. If you simply pay attention, you would think that Scotland is one land mass. But when you really focus, you'll notice that Scotland is also comprised of 780 islands.

If you simply pay attention, you would think that Australia's Great Barrier Reef is 1,256 miles long. But when you really focus, you'll discover that the Great Barrier Reef is also 1,650 feet thick. If you simply pay attention, you would think that the Pacific Ocean entrance to the Panama Canal is west of the Atlantic Ocean entrance. But when you really focus, you'll see that the Pacific Ocean entrance is 27 miles *east* of the Atlantic Ocean entrance.

If you simply pay attention to the Southern Alps of New Zealand, you would see 10 mountains each topping 10,000 feet. But when you really focus, you'll observe that there are also 20 sheep for every person living in New Zealand.   And in the United States, if you simply pay attention, you would think that Nevada is east of California. But when you really focus, you'll notice that Reno, Nevada is actually north *west* of Los Angeles, California.   Stay focused to get a GRIP on your dream.

Tunnel Vision

It's too easy to get stuck in our thinking "tunnels," where our vision is blurred at best and barred at worst to new ideas. Our attention spans are virtually locked in these tunnels, confining our thinking to only what we already know rather than to something new. As a result, we jump to conclusions—and stay where we are.

Consider how quickly customers in a check-cashing store in Spokane, Washington jumped to an erroneous conclusion. They looked up at a television monitor and thought they were witnessing a crime on the premises. They saw a gunman sneaking around. A woman called the police, who later discovered the gunman was actually an actor. The TV monitor was tuned to a daytime TV show.

Tunnel vision can also blind. Most birds will pay attention to their young only when they are in the nest. Out of the nest and beyond their tunnel vision, the birds ignore their young. The cuckoo bird leverages this tunnel vision. It will lay its eggs in the nests of other birds. Since the cuckoo bird is usually larger than other birds, once it is hatched, it kicks the original birds out the nest. Surprisingly, the parent birds start feeding the cuckoo and ignore their own young. They are paying attention to only what's in the nest!

Are you paying too much attention to what's in the nest of your life instead of *what's next* in your life? Are you focused on where you're going?

It is sometimes easy to get unfocused, especially when we're excited about the moment. Consider the US Air Force fighter pilot who was too busy paying attention to the excitement of being at the controls of a $32 million F-15 fighter jet during a training mission. His misdirected attention cost nearly $1 million in damage, and could have cost precious human lives when he inadvertently fired a live missile at another US plane over Anchorage, Alaska.

Are you paying too much attention to what's in the nest of your life instead of *what's next* in your life?

The pilot didn't realize the live missile was on board, even though the missile was clearly marked as such in a maintenance log that is required reading for all pilots before taking off. The pilot absentmindedly wound his thoughts like a coiled Slinky toy around his limited attention span. And like the Slinky, we can only uncoil or react in one way.

How do you react to setting your goals? Do you have a short attention span that could cause you to overlook something or someone important in your achieving them? Or is your attention fully focused on what you need to know and do to make your goals a reality? Are you ready to do whatever it takes to get the results you want?

Information Overload

Unfortunately, many of us are too easily drenched in a flood of information to really take the time to stop and think about right now, this moment.

Here's an activity to show you what effect information overload may be having on you. Do it right now! Put this book down for 30 seconds. Close your eyes. And, no fair peeking! Now think about this moment. Really think. Block out anything else and everything else. And concentrate. Reflect on how you are going to implement the ideas in this book. Ah, Ah, Ah, no daydreaming! Focus right now. And think, no matter how bombarded you are with other information fighting for your attention. Close your eyes tighter and tighter and concentrate harder and harder.

The flood of information can wash away your dreams.

Now that you've opened your eyes again, you've just experienced firsthand how challenging it can be to filter your thinking streams. You now have a better understanding that in setting your goals and making your risks, you need to build barriers against the rivers of negative or useless information flooding into your life. By doing so, you can better sift out and focus on what is important now. You must recognize how formidable those flooding waters of information can be. They have the power to wash away your dreams—if you let them.

Beware of the following kind of information overload when getting a GRIP on your dream:

Research shows that every day the typical American is exposed to 3,000 commercial messages. Every year Americans send nearly a trillion messages, including 600 billion telephone calls, 250 billion memos, 125 billion first class letters and a billion telegrams. And what about the billions of e-mails? There are 1,300 different brands of shampoos, 250 different brands of soda and 200 different brands of cereal.

In 1965, a mechanic could fix any car on the road if he or she understood 5,000 pages of service manuals. By 1990, the mechanic had to wrestle with 93 times more information in 465,000 pages, the equivalent of 250 big-city telephone books.

In 1755, there were 58,000 words listed in Samuel Johnson's first dictionary. Today the number of English words listed in dictionaries has increased to more than 700,000. And in the fourth century, the world's most comprehensive library in Alexandria, Egypt had 700,000 scrolls of information. Today the Library of Congress in Washington, D.C. has more than 80 million items. It has over 500 miles of shelves holding more than 18 million books.

That stream of information is so deep and our attention span so fragmented that a comic strip creator came up with an innovative way to hold a college audience's attention. He sought to make the 20-minute lecture length more durable, so he told his audience to think of his speech as if it were the equivalent of four music videos.   He put his information through a filter his audience could focus on.

Adopt a sense of urgency!

In this chapter you learned the importance of focusing your efforts over and beyond your obstacles—not against them. You also discovered how focusing helps you come closer to achieving your goals. And you learned how important it is to stop the flow of information so that you can better focus on your goals.

But to really *Persist* in getting a GRIP on your dream, you need to do much more than just focus. You need to adopt a sense of urgency, as you'll learn in the next chapter.

Chapter 12

GRIPPING

The Sands of Time

A number of centuries ago, a political leader rose at 4 a.m. every day. He called meetings while still in his bedclothes. He often worked 14 hours a day. Are you paying too much attention to how little time you have to work when getting a GRIP on your dream?

The truth is, you have all the time there is. There is no more. You can't buy it; you can only invest it. You can't create it; you can only leverage it. You can't store it; you can only seize it.

It's no wonder the most effective goal-setters and risk-makers see more congruence than coincidence in the wordplay between won and now. Won spelled backwards is NOW!

With a focus on the NOW, you are in control. You realize and actualize the power that is in your GRIP—a power that is at your fingertips. In fact, that power is under your finger right now.

Take a look at your index finger and say to yourself:

The shadow by my finger cast
Divides the future from the past
Behind its unreturning line,
The vanished hour no longer thine.

Before it lies the unknown hour.
In darkness and beyond thine power.
One hour alone is in thine hands,
The now on which the shadow stands.

That inscription on the sundial of a college campus captures the essence of this chapter. You need to act now to set your goals and make your risks so you can get a better GRIP on your dream.

With a focus on the now, you will be able to keep your Train of Thought on track. You will be able to see your goals as something you link to a *due to* list rather than something you are supposed *to do*.

With a focus on the now, you will spin your Wheel of Personal Fortune with more authority and without distraction.

With a focus on the now, you will more effectively write your own OBIT—your *Optimum Behavior Information Transfer*. You will more readily rocket your goals, boosting them like monuments higher and higher on a pedestal of responsibility. You will recognize your you-niqueness and have the courage to stand in public in your BVDs—your *Beliefs, Values and Disciplines*.

With a focus on the now, you will more easily engage in the five-step GOALS process of *Gestation, Observation, Activation, Legislation and Stimulation*.

With a focus on the now, you will more readily be able to make a RISK—a *Revised Insight Stimulating Knowledge*.

With a focus on the now, you will more aggressively adopt the seven strategies to PREPARE your goals: **P**urpose, **R**eflection, **E**xpectation, **P**enciling, **A**nticipation, **R**eading and **E**xpansion.

With a focus on the now, you will be more prepared to see yourself as *forte* not simply forty.

With a focus on the now, you will be able to get a GRIP on a more powerful process of *Goal-setting, Risk-making, Initiating and Persisting.* You will be able to discover a treasure chest filled with $86,400 every day. That's what happens when you GRIP the sands of time, as if you were getting $1 for each second of your 24-hour day.

To get a GRIP on your dream you have to acknowledge the power of time. Maybe that's why Marie Antoinette received 51 decorative watches as engagement presents. Maybe that's why *not even* the most powerful person in the world can manufacture an antique in a few days. And maybe that's why even the most gifted artist cannot paint a masterpiece in just a few weeks. It takes time—a long, long time.

Time isn't something you serve like a prisoner, mark like a musician, or record like an historian.

Time is something you need to *invest* like a banker. Cash in on your time. GRIP those sands of time before they slip entirely through the hourglass of your life. Use your time *right now* to get a GRIP on your dream. Yearn to earn, and make your dreams *more* than just something you want to come true. Focus and make them come *due*.

Epilogue

The GRIP System

Movie buffs know that a grip is a technician who grips the lights, the cameras or the scenery to move them around for proper illustration of the scene. When you implement the GRIP system of—*Goal-Setting, Risk-Making, Initiating and Persisting*—you need to become even more adept at gripping the light in your life so it guides you on your path of success. You also need to grip the scenery in your life so you can play your role with passion.

Think of the GRIP system as a process that sparks a more flexible, dynamic, powerful personal leadership in your career or business, in your relationships and in all other parts of your life. With this system, you can GRIP your dream. With this GRIP system, you can bridge the gap from where you are to where you want to be. You can connect the parts of your life into a more viable, enriching, rewarding whole.

Consider this GRIP system as a series of bridges that connect your life to your dreams, much like the 65 bridges that connect the five boroughs of New York City into a more vibrant, viable, vital whole. Use this system as a bridge that will help you conquer your self-imposed limitations, much like the Romans conquered the world. They built 2,000 bridges to link 52,000 miles of roads, which helped them pave the way for the rise of the Roman Empire. Use this system as a bridge to pave the way to build your own personal empire.

The bridge metaphor is particularly apt. Author Fraser P. Seitel agrees. He quoted me in his 1994 textbook, *The Practice of Public Relations* (fifth edition). Seitel writes: "One public relations professional who probably summed up the opinion of many colleagues about exactly what it is he does for a living was Peter F. Jeff, a Michigan practitioner who wrote the following to a local editor."

"A Public relations professional is a bridge builder, not a drum beater, building long-term relationships between an organization or company and its publics based on two-way communications (i.e. listening and speaking). A public relations professional serves as an interpreter, helping the organization or company adapt and adjust to the political, social and economic climate…and assisting the public in more fully understanding the company."

As the author of *Get A GRIP On Your Dream,* I attempted to *leverage* that same discipline. I wanted to serve as an interpreter between you and your dreams, to help you bridge the gap between where you are and where you want to be, and to help you get a stronger GRIP on your personal leadership. To help you do that, review the GRIP Steps and then apply the GRIP Tools.

GRIP Steps

A Step by Step Summary of Using the GRIP System

GOAL-SETTING

1. Write your OBIT *(Optimum Biographical Information Transfer)*.
2. Define your VALUES (*Vital Assessment Leveraging Unique Expectations Systematically*).
3. Spin your WHEEL OF PERSONAL FORTUNE.
4. Define your *due to* List.
5. Develop your goals with WISDOM so they are *Written, Incremental, Specific, Deadline oriented, Opportunistic and Measurable.*
6. Use the 5-step **GOALS** process in setting your goals *(Gestation, Observation, Activation, Legislation and Stimulation)*.

RISK-MAKING

7. In achieving your goals, think of RISK as a *Revised Insight Stimulating Knowledge.*
8. Failure isn't for failures. Think of failure as a learning experience and—*fail your way to success!*
9. In making a RISK (you never take a risk), be willing to challenge your previous perception and perspective on your world.

INITIATING

10. Change your seat in the theater of life. Remember, how you stand on an issue depends where you are sitting.
11. Align your dreams with your sense of integrity to make a more viable RISK. With integrity comes a sense of passionate responsibility.
12. Don't lie down on the procrustean bed (a habit or rut into which someone is forced). Leverage your you-niqueness in reaching your dreams. Follow your own chosen path.
13. **PREPARE** yourself. Use Prepare as an acronym for developing your dreams with *Purpose, Reflection, Expectation, Penciling Anticipation, Reading and Expansion.*

PERSISTING

14. Don't let circumstances (your age, your education or whatever) deter or defer your dreams. Follow your dream and it'll take you where you're supposed to go.

15. You're never too old, too young, too tall, too short, too experienced or too inexperienced. If you're in or near your 40s, think of yourself as in your *forte!*
16. Focus on your sense of purpose to keep yourself on track with your goals.
17. Create a sense of urgency. Do it now! Remember that Won spelled backwards is Now.

Practice Using *The GRIP System*— and Most of All, Use the Tool on the Next Page...

How To Get Your Best GRIP

The Most Important Tool of All

Spin your Wheel of Personal Fortune, and determine precisely what your *yearning* is. Is it a new house? How about a new car? Could it be a successful business that doubles its revenues in a specific time period? Might it be a college education for your children? What about increased health and vigor to enjoy your life more fully?

Review the Wheel of Personal Fortune in Chapter One. Select one of the icons (pictures) that best describes the value inherent in your *dream,* which enables you to get your best GRIP. Simply put, your dream is the best tool you can use to get you into action.

The Wheel of Personal Fortune features a picture of a graduation cap representing an educational goal, a picture of the medical symbol of intertwined snakes representing a health goal, and a picture of cash, a home and a car representing financial goals. If none of these work for you, insert your own icon—the one that best represents the value of the dream you are getting a GRIP on. Then describe the icon on your Wheel of Personal Fortune in one word and write it on several 3x5 index cards.

This one word represents your goals—*purposefully, passionately and personally.* Focus on it until it boils inside you and bubbles to the top in a specific time period. And keep the heat of your passion on. Then your goals and dreams will *come due,* rather than just become something else for you *to do.*

Limit your *due to* to the one item that's most important to you. Place the 3X5 index cards where you can easily see them—on your refrigerator, bathroom mirror, car dash, office desk, or work station. Look at them often, as lovingly as you do the pictures of your family.

Passionately *infuse* your dream into your brain and heart, and make it come alive with purposeful action!

Rocketing Your Goals

Blast Off Towards Your Dream

Ｉt's as easy as 1-2-3 to rocket your goals higher in your business or career, in your relationships, and in the rest of your life. Build your goals the way a rocket is built—in stages. Use the rocket illustration in Chapter One to carefully define your goal with an overriding *due to* purpose, then provide booster rockets—specific stages—to propel your goals toward success.

1 Review the Wheel of Personal Fortune in Chapter One. Determine the personal value you *yearn* for. Visualize it so well that you can see it coming *due* to you. Think about the one-word description of the icon you selected (or

created) on the Wheel of Personal Fortune. Inscribe the word on the rocket's capsule. Think of this word as your value statement—the one which will "program" your capsule to stay on course. Then, no matter how much the topsy-turvy world of people, with their own agendas, may try to spin your life out of control, you'll be as solid as a rock.

2 Add thrust to your goal by giving yourself an exact timeframe in which you intend to accomplish a specific task in support of that goal. This second stage will then take your goal to a higher altitude.

3 Add even more thrust by determining one specific thing you can do in the next three days to reach your goal. This third stage of the rocket will vault you toward your dreams and put you in orbit!

And now you are ready to…

"Get
a GRIP
on
your dream
and
make it
come
due!"

About the Author

Peter Jeff is a professional speaker specializing in personal leadership, creative thinking and effective communications. He is the president of *The LeaderShip Company,* a personal development company in Grand Rapids, Michigan that helps people chart their own dreams on the seas of change. He provides keynote presentations and seminars that help people in organizations more effectively create, collaborate and communicate.

Peter is known as *The GRIP Guy* for his signature message of helping people get a **GRIP** on their dreams through a personal leadership system of *Goal-Setting, Risk-Making, Initiating and Persisting.* He is a dynamic and entertaining speaker who parlays more than 25 years of professional communications experience into his writing and speaking. He lives with his wife, Deborah, and their children, Amy and Laura, in Grand Rapids, Michigan. E-mail The GRIP Guy at gripguy@attbi.com; phone 616-455-GRIP or 616-455-4747; fax 616-455-2722; Website www.gripleadership.com.